It's Just a Game!

Youth, Sports & Self Esteem:

A Guide for Parents

It's Just a Game!

Youth, Sports & Self Esteem: A Guide for Parents

Darrell J. Burnett, Ph.D.

Authors Choice Press
San Jose New York Lincoln Shanghai

It's Just a Game!
Youth, Sports & Self Esteem: A Guide for Parents

Authors Choice Press
an imprint of iUniverse.com, Inc.

For information address:
iUniverse.com, Inc.
5220 S 16th, Ste. 200
Lincoln, NE 68512
www.iuniverse.com

Originally published by Masters Press

Interior photos by Dr. Darrell J. Burnett, with the exception of the "About the Author" photo, by John Jupiter, and the basketball and hockey action photos, By RSP Photo.

Back cover photo of Dr. Burnett by RSB Photo.

Cover graphic design by David Bird Studio.

Cover photo provided by the National Youth Sports Coaches Association.

ISBN: 0-595-16364-5

Printed in the United States of America

FOREWORD: AUTHOR'S NOTES ON REVISED EDITION

A Title Change

In this revised edition, I changed the original title, *Youth, Sports, & Self Esteem: A Guide for Parents*, to a subtitle, and titled the book, **It's Just a Game!**

Here's why. Since the book's original publishing in 1993 the world of youth sports has continued to draw the attention of the media. In recent years, episodes of parental overreaction and overinvolvement in youth sports have been documented in newspapers, magazines, TV/Radio talk shows, and internet chat rooms. Many Youth Sports organizations are requiring parents to attend "sportsmanship" workshops as a condition for registering their kids to play youth sports. In many cases, part of the registration involves a parental signature whereby a parent agrees to abide by codes of appropriate conduct at youth sports events, with consequences for misconduct.

I have had numerous media interviews asking me why there seems to be an increase in unsportsmanlike conduct among adults at youth league games. My response is that, in many cases, youth league games are no longer <u>games</u>. If a youth league game is a game, then the atmosphere is one of fun and an opportunity to learn some skills. A mistake during a game is seen as an opportunity to learn and improve. If, on the other hand, a youth league game is seen as a possible ticket to an eventual college scholarship and perhaps a life as a professional athlete, then the atmosphere is tense, leading to possible emotional overreaction by a parent if a youngster makes a mistake, an official "blows" a call, or a coach plays favorites. In my opinion, we, as parents, have to remember that, when it comes to youth sports, it's just a game. I changed my title to reflect my conviction.

Some Additional Items

After two printings of my original book I wanted to update a few things, while leaving the original text of the book in tact. So, I've updated the ABOUT THE AUTHOR information, and added a few items (checklists, references, etc.) by placing them in the AFTERWORD section after the text of the original book.

Since my original publishing, the world of youth hockey has expanded significantly. In response, I've added a skills checklist and a positive behavior checklist for youth hockey.

As mentioned above, the topic of "sportsmanship" has become a major issue in youth sports since my original publication, so I've added my <u>Sportsmanship Checklists</u> for players and parents, and my 10-item "Sideline Suggestions" which I wrote originally for the **Playbook for Kids:** *A Parent's Guide to Help Kids Get the Most Out of Sports*, published by the Gatorade Company in 1999.

In addition, I've added a few more references.

Darrell J. Burnett, Ph.D.

Special Thanks to:

Holly Kondras, for her diligence and patience in editing the manuscript.

Rancho Niguel, California Little League, Division 55, for promoting an atmosphere of positive coaching, fun, and games, and for encouraging me to put my ideas into writing.

All the parents and kids in the photos, whose exuberance, joy, and excitement helped capture the spirit of the book.

Contents

Dedication

To my kids, Matt, Tom, and Jill; my wife, Susann; all the kids I've coached; my special grade school coach, Dan Finley, who knows all about helping kids in sports; and all parents who, like my own, have sacrificed their time to help their kids have fun, feel good, and learn skills in youth sports.

Introduction

In the 20 years I have been working with kids and families as a psychologist, *self esteem* has been one of the most frequently requested topics in my parenting workshops. In my private practice, behind closed doors in my office, when kids start talking, self esteem becomes a major topic.

In my experience with troubled teenagers over the years, I have found that a high percentage of them started "feeling bad" from their early years as a child. As they relate their negative memories of childhood, there is often "something missing." That "something," in my experience, is often the fun and good times connected with youth sports.

As I sit and listen to them talk about how they "dropped out" of organized sports in their early childhood because of negative experiences (pressure, embarrassment, yelling coaches, screaming parents), I feel a sense of frustration that, at a time in their early lives when they should have been having fun and playing games, these kids experienced only feelings of rejection and hurt.

As a psychologist, a father of three active participants in youth sports, and a youth sports coach, I was approached by our local youth sports board to speak at coaching clinics about "positive coaching," with an emphasis on having fun. Out of those clinics came a series of booklets for youth sports coaches, briefly summarizing some psychological points to remember when working with kids in sports so that, as coaches, we don't lose sight of the real purpose of youth sports: having fun!

This book is an expansion of those booklets, with the added dimension of how the development of self esteem is such an integral part of youth sports. This book is written just for *parents*. I realize that most coaches are parents, and I hope that they will find the book helpful in that capacity as well. However, I am writing this, as a parent, for all parents of youth leaguers, to talk about the power we have, as parents, to use youth sports as an opportunity for developing self confidence and self esteem in our kids.

Athletics: A Source of Self Esteem

It has been said that, for kids, there are three main areas which most affect their self confidence, their self esteem, and their view of themselves:

1. Physical appearance

2. Intelligence

3. Athletics

As parents, we all go through the struggle of helping our kids cope with the physical appearance hassles. (" I can't get my hair to look right!" "I'm too fat!" "I'm too skinny!" "My nose is too big for my face!" "My ears stick out!" and the list goes on, and on, and on.) We all try to bolster our kids when they doubt their intelligence, stumbling in school with a failed test, a low grade, or embarrassment at being compared to other "smart" kids.

Sometimes, as parents, we may feel helpless to solve the physical appearance problems or the intelligence issues. It's almost as if our kids are going to have to go through periods of being self-critical about their looks or intelligence regardless of what we say or do to try to make it less painful.

However, when it comes to the area of *athletics*, I think parents have a great opportunity to help their kids see themselves in a positive light, regardless of their athletic skills. From the beginning years of T-ball baseball, "beehive" soccer, pee-wee football, or eight foot high basketball rims, all the way through high school sports, there are lots of ways we can help make youth sports a positive experience, enhancing our kids' self image along the way.

As a psychologist, I've seen kids really get down on themselves for "looking funny," or "feeling stupid." However, I've seen those same kids boost themselves up through having fun and developing basic skills in youth sports.

That's what this book is about. It's about how we, as parents, can, with a little effort, do our part to help kids enjoy youth sports, giving them lots of opportunities for *having fun* and *feeling good*. It's about how we can help our kids build good childhood memories, recalling a time in their life which was filled with the joy of playing games.

The first chapter discusses self esteem as it applies to the world of kids. There is a discussion of how youth sports can contribute to the four cornerstones which make up the foundation of a child's self view and self acceptance. The subsequent chapters discuss 12 ways in which parents can act to promote self esteem in their own kids through their youth sports activities. The 12 ways apply on and off the field, but the emphasis in the book is always on sports.

One final note, the book centers on four sports: baseball/softball, basketball, football, and soccer. This is not to slight other sports. It is just that most of my experience has been in dealing with kids who were involved in these organized team sports. Parents with kids involved in other sports (volleyball, golf, hockey, lacrosse, tennis, swimming, etc.) can, in my opinion, apply the same principles. In fact, I would welcome any feedback or communication from parents concerning their experiences in any of these sports.

I. Self Esteem & Youth Sports

"The most important psychological reward offered by sports is the opportunity to experience and build self esteem."

Eric Margenau, Ph.D.

Sports Psychologist

Self Esteem: Definitions

"Self esteem" seems to be the buzzword of the decade: on TV and radio talk shows, in books, in magazine articles, it's hard not to hear something about it everywhere you turn.

Yet, it can be very confusing, because there seem to be many different ways of defining self esteem. The dictionary definition describes self esteem as "belief in oneself; self respect." Overall, when people talk about someone having high self esteem, they usually mean that a person has self acceptance and considers himself/herself worthy of respect and love.

Over the years, researchers have defined self esteem from several vantage points:

- "The extent to which an individual believes himself to be capable, significant, successful, and worthy."

  — Stanley Coopersmith

- "The process of appreciating our own worth and importance, having the character to be accountable for ourselves and to act responsibly toward others."

  — The California Psychologists' Task Force

- "Confidence in one's ability to think, to cope with challenges; confidence in one's right to be happy; the feeling of being worthy, deserving, entitled to assert one's needs and wants and to enjoy the fruits of one's efforts."   — Nathaniel Branden

- "A sense of connectiveness, a sense of uniqueness, a sense of power, a sense of models."

  — Harris Clemes and Reynold Bean

SELF ESTEEM: FOUR CORNERSTONES

However, Denis Waitley seems to summarize all the research best when he describes the four cornerstones of self esteem:

1. A sense of **Belonging**
2. A sense of **Worthiness**
3. A sense of **Dignity**
4. A sense of **Control**

Let's take a brief look at what these four cornerstones are all about.

A Sense of Belonging

Man is a social animal. We need to feel accepted into a social group. And so we tend to look for a *group* which will validate our importance. In most cases, the family is the initial group which helps develop a sense of belonging. If not, another group will be sought out. Gangs, according to sociologists, offer a very strong sense of belonging.

A Sense of Worthiness

Self esteem is self acceptance, as a *person*, worthy of love and caring from others. It should be part of being a person, regardless of looks, talents, skills, or wealth. Unfortunately, many people base their self image on their achievements or

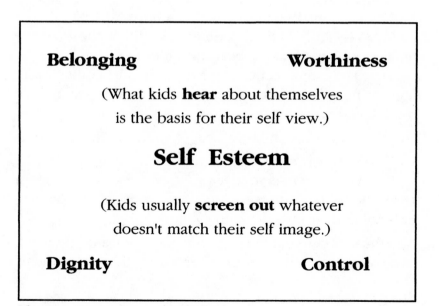

Belonging   **Worthiness**

(What kids **hear** about themselves
is the basis for their self view.)

Self Esteem

(Kids usually **screen out** whatever
doesn't match their self image.)

Dignity   **Control**

The Four Cornerstones of Self Esteem

other things outside themselves as a person. Fallen athletes, former beauty queens, bankrupt money barons, often struggle with self acceptance after their "outside" source of importance has been destroyed.

A Sense of Dignity

Attempts to "break" prisoners-of-war often begin with attempts to strip them of their dignity. Repeated acts of humiliation, degradation, showing little respect for the humanness of the person are aimed at destroying one of the essentials of self esteem: a sense of dignity, as manifested by respect from others. Interactions from others which accord little or no respect to an individual can wear away even the strongest of human beings.

A Sense of Control

Finally, a sense of control is central to self acceptance. Feeling accountable, feeling that you have choices, and the ability to control your environment or destiny; these are the feelings which are at the heart of self esteem. On the other hand, to the extent that you feel at the mercy of others, with little or no power to change your life, to that extent, self esteem decreases significantly.

While parents can't be expected to act as therapists with their kids, I think everyone needs to be aware of these four cornerstones of self esteem and the power parents possess in helping their kids develop in these areas.

As the diagram on the preceding page indicates, there are two essential points to remember about kids' self esteem:

1. Kids' images of themselves are based mainly upon *what they hear about themselves from others*. During the earliest years, the most powerful "others" are the parents.

2. Once children form an image of themselves, they tend to *screen out* whatever doesn't match that image.

It is painfully clear, then, that, as parents, we should weigh our words and actions toward our children so as to promote a sense of belonging, worthiness, dignity, and control. If we do this, we can lay a foundation for a positive self image and self acceptance in our children. If we don't use our power as parents to help build self image and self acceptance, rest assured that someone else will! And that influence may not be a positive one.

Remember that once a child has formed a self image, that child tends to screen out what doesn't fit that image. A kid with a positive self image tends to "screen out" negative attacks and influences, and can handle correction. However, a kid with a negative self image tends to "screen out" positives and becomes preoccupied with negative feelings about self. This is the kid who cannot handle correction, and who is very sensitive to criticism.

Youth Sports: Opportunities to Develop Self Esteem

When you think about it, youth sports offer us a golden opportunity, as parents, to help our kids develop a positive self image by working on the four cornerstones of self esteem: a sense of belonging, worthiness, dignity, and control.

A Sense of Belonging

The concept of teamwork and *team* identity is central to most youth sports. The camaraderie, the team photo, the team uniforms, and the team parties all go a long way towards helping a youngster develop a sense of belonging. As parents, we have repeated opportunities to promote team identity and team spirit.

A Sense of Worthiness

In youth sports, especially in the early years, the emphasis is on the philosophy that "everybody plays." This teaches youngsters to identify themselves as players, not as winners or losers. It implies that their worth is intact just as *participants*, who do their best, accept their mistakes, accept loss, and still maintain a solid positive identity. On the other hand, if there is constant pressure to "win or else," it can take its toll. Once again, as parents, we can help set the tone that participation is what counts in youth sports. (**The Positive Behavior Checklists** in the Appendix emphasize participation, regardless of specific skills.)

A Sense of Dignity

In youth sports, if the emphasis is on positives, such as having fun, feeling good, and developing skills, there will be no room for put-downs, rude remarks, or sarcasm from adults in charge or in the stands. As parents, we can be models of *respect* for the kids, helping them as supportive and encouraging adults.

A Sense of Control

And finally, in youth sports, youngsters have the opportunity to develop a sense of control, learning skills in each sport to the best of their ability, building confidence as they see progress in skill building, and in becoming accountable for their actions, especially in the area of sportsmanship.

Sportsmanship after the game

Parents play a vital role in their children's participation in Youth League. From the day our kids attend their first practice session, we need to be aware of how we can use sports to help build self esteem. We need to recognize the power we have in helping our kids. Finally, we need to realize the importance of our *active* participation in making youth sports a positive experience. The years of youth sports are a golden opportunity. They pass too quickly, and once they are gone, they're gone for good.

In the rest of the book, we are going to discuss 12 specific ways that we parents can take active steps in helping our kids experience youth sports as a time for having fun, feeling good, and developing skills. As a memory aid, just think of the phrase: **K-I-D-S I-N S-P-O-R-T-S.**

1. **K**eep it positive.
2. **I**nstill laughter and humor.
3. **D**evelop team spirit.
4. **S**tep into their shoes.

5. **I**nvolve yourself.
6. **N**otice any and all progress.

7. **S**how excitement and enthusiastic praise.
8. **P**raise specifics.
9. **O**ffer a good example.
10. **R**emember to have fun.
11. **T**each Skills.
12. **S**et reasonable expectations.

II. Keep it Positive

"I just got tired of all the criticism and yelling. It seemed like all I ever heard was what I was doing wrong. My parents kept a 'report card' on each game, telling me all my mistakes. I felt like crying, but I just held it in. I tried hard, but it seemed like whatever I did, it just wasn't enough for them."

—A nine year old boy, explaining why he quit playing organized sports

Accentuate the Positive

One of the most key ingredients in promoting self esteem in the Youth Leaguer is for parents to concentrate on *positives*. This seems obvious, but I can't tell you how many kids I've seen whose parents were just like the ones mentioned in the above quote from the unfortunate nine year old.

Why is this so important? Because, as we mentioned in the opening chapter, kids' self esteem is based mainly on what they hear about themselves from others, especially parents. The earlier a child hears positives about himself/herself, the better the chance of a positive self image.

In a healthy family, there should be a **four-to-one** ratio of positive to negative remarks. That is, for every critical or corrective remark, there should be four encouraging remarks or "pats on the back." Correction is important, but encouragement should be the norm. Ask yourself, when you think of your kid as an athlete, do you think more negatives than positives? Are you spending more time correcting what you perceive as mistakes, rather than encouraging your kid just for *participating*? Sometimes, parents get locked into the criticism trap with our kids in sports, constantly correcting them, showing them the "right" way to do something (hold the bat, throw the ball, kick the ball, or shoot the ball), instead of just letting them enjoy the thrill of playing. It's ok to teach skills, but kids learn better from positives than from negative criticism.

The majority of kids whom I see in my practice as a psychologist are very sensitive to criticism because, in most cases, they haven't received much positive attention. Consequently, their self confidence and self image are low, they are quick to doubt themselves, and they are quick to pick up on anything "negative" that is said to them.

The world of youth sports should be an arena for heaping positives on each and every kid playing. Kids will experience plenty of criticism as they grow up. They can use all the positives they can get. What better place to go for positives than on a playing field, where the main emphasis is fun and games.

ANDY CAPP

(Reprinted with special permission from North America Syndicate, Inc.)

Look for the Positives

As parents, we would do well to imitate Flo, the comic strip character in *ANDY CAPP*. As seen in the comic strip, she forces herself to *find something to praise* in Andy. So, she ignores the messy room and concentrates instead on the clean ceiling!

We have to look for and find something to praise when our kid is involved in sports. This can be quite a challenge at times, especially on those days when our kid is "out of it." But, once again, recognizing our power as parents, and our role in promoting positive self confidence in our kids, we've got to be creative. **The Positive Behavior Checklists** in the Appendix point out several positive behaviors which can be praised, regardless of skills. For example, regardless of whether a kid is hitting well (in baseball), he/she can be praised for hustling on and off the field.

You might like to go over the lists in the Appendix and see how many you have already noticed in your kid. The **86 Ways To Say "Very Good"** is another interesting checklist for us as parents. How many of the 86 have you used with your kid? Go over the lists, take them to the game, and yell them out! (In Chapter VII we'll discuss lots of ways to notice positive progress in our kids.)

Eliminate the Negative

Did you ever notice how some people are preoccupied with finding and emphasizing *negatives* in their environment? They seem to be experts in playing the game of "Let's find the flaw!" They're the ones who see the glass as half-empty rather than half-filled. In youth sports activities, their negativity can often take the form of harsh criticism toward their kids or others. It seems obvious, but we need to remind ourselves that put-downs and sarcastic remarks have no place in our interactions with our kids. Words like"loser" or "clumsy" can be devastating to some kids. However, I hear negative remarks only too often. I was having dinner with a family one evening when their thirteen year old son came rushing in the door, full of excitement and waving a red ribbon. He proudly announced that his four-man relay team had won first place at the swimming meet. His dad remarked, "It's a good thing the other three guys on your team are fast swimmers!" The boy's face lost its smile, and his head dropped to his chest. The dad said he was only kidding, but the damage had already been done.

The following verbatim samples of damaging negative remarks speak for themselves. In my opinion, some come close to verbal abuse!

- 'If you had your eye on the ball out there in the outfield, instead of picking your nose and waving to your friend at the snack shop, you could have caught that fly ball, and you wouldn't have caused your team to lose!"

    — A father to his seven year old T-Ball Little Leaguer

- "Quit running away from the ball! Go to the ball! If you can't be aggressive, you may as well quit right now"

    — A father to his seven year old daughter at a soccer game

- "This is soccer, not basketball, can't you remember to keep your hands off the ball? Do I have to tape your hands to your sides?"

    — A father to his eight year old son at a soccer game

- "If you made both of those free throws we would have won. Now we've got to go to overtime, thanks to you!"

    — A father to his nine year old son who had just made one of two free throws to tie the game for his basketball team at the end of regulation time

Sports can be such a positive experience for kids, really helping them feel good about themselves. I cite these negative examples so that we can spend our energy as parents avoiding the harping, the complaining, the yelling, the lecturing, and all the other things we might be tempted to do as parents when we go to our kids' games or practice. If we put all our energy into positives with our kids in sports, we can help them see themselves as winners, regardless of athletic skills or team standings. As parents, we've got to minimize criticism, and seize every opportunity to smother our kids with encouragement and positives, so that when inevitable disappointments or mistakes occur in the game or practice, they'll have the self confidence to handle them.

Pat McInally, former National Football League player, who is now a columnist and an author of an excellent book for parents on the topic of youth sports, feels that, when parents go to their kids' games, there should be no room for negatives. He advises parents to try to be positive all the time! If you're looking for a good general guideline on how to act at your kids' games, follow his advice:

*"I believe young athletes should be **praised** when they do well, **encouraged** when they err, and **consoled** when they make major blunders or lose tough contests."*

III. Instill Laughter & Humor

"He who laughs — lasts."

Norwegian Proverb

If there's a single quality in kids with low self esteem, it seems to be that they take themselves too seriously. They *seem to have an absence of a sense of humor. They seldom* laugh.

If you're looking for what characteristics to teach your kids give them *laughter,* a sense of *humor,* and a love of *play.*

Over the past two years, I have been giving workshops in classrooms at the Elementary, Junior High, and High School levels. Each year, the schools poll the kids on topics they would like to discuss. One of the most popularly requested topics over the past two years has been "stress management." Remember that this is not corporate America, this is the classroom! Kids are increasingly reporting that they are feeling "stress" in one way or another, with an increase in the number of worries and pressures at the elementary level! I have seen two ten-year-olds with complaints of ulcers.

Anything we can do to "lighten up" our kids will help. Fortunately, research shows that laughter and a sense of humor are great stress relievers. Denis Waitley refers to research which describes how laughter and smiling set off specific chemical reactions in the brain which promote increased healing and decreased depression. He notes that studies have shown that laughter and humor promote creative problem solving and increased learning. Norman Cousins wrote of how he used laughter as a healing mechanism for cancer.

Where better to emphasize laughter and a sense of humor than at youth sports, where the whole atmosphere is "fun and games?" Besides, laughter and a sense of humor often make for better athletes. Why? When kids are playing sports, laughing and smiling tend to add to their relaxation, which can add to productivity and may often enhance their performance. Of course, we're not advocating that every kid play the "clown," but we are talking about trying to keep our kids from getting so serious that they lose the joy of playing.

The "Lighter Side" of Youth Sports:
An Antidote to Pressure

It is very important for us, as parents of youth league players, to make sure our kids see the lighter side of sports and not get weighed down with self imposed pressure. Everyone was alarmed recently when a 15 year old boy apparently took his life after completing a baseball tournament. A note said that he just couldn't handle the pressure. Granted, this is rare, but it points out the potential *pressure* that kids can put themselves under in youth sports. As parents, we not only have to avoid putting undue pressure on our kids in sports, we have to take active steps to help keep things light. All we have to do is look through newspaper articles, and we'll find story after story of players who put pressure on themselves and take youth sports too seriously. Here are just a few stories I read in newspaper articles over the past year.

One story told of a boy, age 11, who had always been the "star" of the team. Everyone expected him to win every game he pitched. After a season of successes, he entered the playoffs and gave up seven runs in the first inning. The teammates were stunned, and so was he. He said he had come to the point where he was afraid to come to the ball park because all he thought about was whether he would live up to everyone's expectations. He said he had lost his sense of humor. His parents had noticed his recent serious-ness, but they thought it was just a "phase" he was going through.

Another story told of a ten year old boy who cried and walked off the field, refusing to play the rest of the game, after a girl hit his pitch for a homerun.

Still another story told of a ten year old soccer goalkeeper who played a magnificent game with several outstanding saves. However, it was a semi-final game in a tournament, and it went into overtime and eventually to a "shoot out" wherein each team has five players who get a "free kick" on goal. The goalkeeper did another magnificent job, beating the odds and blocking two of the five attempted kicks. However, his teammates on offense missed three attempted kicks, and they lost the game. He burst into tears and blamed himself, saying that he had let his teammates down. All efforts by his teammates, coaches, and parents to comfort him were unsuccessful.

These examples of self imposed pressure highlight the kids who need to be reminded of the "lighter" side of youth sports. Granted, there are going to be times when laughter and humor are tough to pull off, and times when the kids have to experience the sadness and disappointment which comes with competitive sports. Our goal, as parents, should be to try to keep our kids from placing pressure on themselves and to keep things as light and humorous as we can. It's sometimes a challenge for us, but I've seen some real creativity in quite a few parents.

Keeping the "Lighter Side" in Focus: Case Studies

There are lots of ways to keep things light, even when misfortune strikes. The following are examples which I personally have witnessed. I'm sure we can all add to the list from our own experience.

I know one dad who finds it helpful to remind his kids that professional athletes keep a sense of humor and are able to laugh at themselves. Dad keeps a library of videotapes (*Football Follies, Baseball Bloopers,* and the like), and gets them out to watch with his kids whenever they seem to be getting too serious or too upset about an error, a missed shot, or a blown assignment. He also reminds them that each professional team usually has a prankster or a clown in the clubhouse. He has videotaped interviews of professional athletes who talk about using humor as a way of keeping "loose" and fighting off the tension of big league competition.

One baseball team was losing. In the top of the first inning the opposing visiting team scored five runs without getting an out. As the home team came into the dugout for the bottom half of the first inning, most of the kids sat down on the bench with their heads hung down. However, the nine year old pitcher, who had been unable to get anybody out, said, "Thank God for the five run limit rule!" The kids looked at the coach, who smiled, and everyone laughed. They went on to enjoy the game (even though they lost).

Another baseball team was losing by ten runs. They were the visiting team, which meant that the home team would probably not have to bat in the last inning. One of the eight year olds said, "Look at it this way. The game will be shorter, and we'll get our snacks sooner." Everyone laughed and, again, enjoyed the rest of the game.

A mother noticed a muddy pool of water in the corner of the soccer field, due to a broken sprinkler. She warned her seven year old son to watch out for it. He promptly turned to his teammates and said, "Hey guys, there's a mud puddle down in the corner of the field! Make sure we kick the ball over there so we can splash!" The kids saw their coach grin at the remark, and, sure enough, it didn't take long for the teams to head for the "mud bowl" in the corner. Needless to say, they loved it! The mom and coach realized that, at that age, the kids were more into the fun of playing than the end product of scoring.

A soccer team of ten and eleven year old boys was named "The Untouchables." After their first game, which resulted in a six to two loss, someone asked the name of the team. One boy said, "We're 'The Untouchables'!" Another teammate replied, "Not anymore," and noted that they had been "touched" for six goals. Everyone laughed, and ten minutes later, they were playing videogames at the pizza parlor.

A soccer coach was having trouble getting his 7 year olds to concentrate on practicing shots on goal during practice. He came up with a gimmick. He made paper "bullseye" targets and hooked them on to the back of the pants of the other coach and three parent onlookers at practice. The coach then lined up the four adults at the goal with their backs to the kids and challenged his players to "hit the bullseye" with their kicks on goal. Laughter filled the air, and the coach had no further trouble getting the kids to practice their kicks. (All adults escaped unharmed!)

A ten year old boy was playing point guard in basketball. There were only a few seconds left in the game, and his team was winning by three points. The coach wanted to run out the clock because the other team was out of time outs. He yelled out to the boy to "take his time" bringing the ball upcourt. The boy thought he heard the coach say to "call time," so he called "time out," with five seconds left on the clock which created a chance for the opposing team to steal the ball on an inbounds pass. The boy was being yelled at by the other kids on the team. He was on the verge of tears. The coach saw it and tried to lighten up the tense situation. He turned to the boy and said, "Well, at least you heard the word 'time.' That's 50% of the message. That proves you were listening rather than daydreaming about our pizza party after we win this game! In fact, I'm glad we've got this time out, so I can tell you guys what a great game you've played. Now here's the inbound play..." The boy relaxed, grinned, made a perfect inbounds pass to an open player, and time ran out.

An eight year old girl on a basketball team had long shoestrings that continually came undone during the game. Afterwards, her dad took her out for an ice cream sundae to celebrate her award for setting a new record for "the most time-outs to tie her shoes!" She loved it, and her mom shortened the shoestrings for the next game.

At the beginning of a basketball game, a father was yelling at his nine year old son to keep "both hands up" on defense. The boy had one hand up and the other at his side. As the dad yelled, the boy had an anguished look on his face. As Dad continued yelling, the boy finally put both hands up, and his basketball trunks fell to his ankles! It seems it was the first game of the season, and uniforms were given out at the game. He was a "small," but they only had a "large." He had been keeping one hand near his trunks to keep them up. The coach called time out. A mother in the stands had a safety pin, and the coach pinned the trunks to make them fit. The parents in the stands applauded, and the boy grinned and went on to finish the game with both hands up on defense. After the game, his dad bought him a pack of basketball cards for the "Outstanding performance under duress" award. His dad told him he won the award "hands down!" (The boy got "small" trunks before the next game!)

One team had a "laughter" award at the end of the season for the kid who was able to maintain a healthy sense of humor all season. The kids knew about the award at the beginning of the season, and they all kept involved in trying to win it. The parents were aware of it, and they took turns tallying the sense of humor incidents through out the season. It was a great season for everyone.

The stories are endless and refreshing. It is amazing how creative we can be as adults if we put our efforts toward helping our kids "lighten up" in youth sports activities. We have to continually remind ourselves and our kids that *there is life after youth sports*! If we find ourselves taking the whole youth sports thing too seriously, we're likely to convey this to our kids. Remember, we're the role models. If something funny happens, notice it and join in the laughter. If you get an opportunity to lighten things up, do it! We're building memories for our kids. Let's make them positive happy ones. Let's help keep the pressure off. Let's keep the laughter and humor going.

IV. Develop Team Spirit

"I've never been on a team before, with uniforms, and a team picture, and a team banner. The other kids' parents even know my name!"

— An eight year old soccer player

Youth Sports: A Sense of Belonging

In the opening chapter, we talked about the sense of *belonging* as a major cornerstone in building self esteem. We noted that kids will meet that need to belong in any way they can. Gang activity has been cited as meeting a strong, previously unmet need to belong. Youth sports, with its emphasis upon teamwork and team identity, is a great place for a kid to develop a strong sense of belonging, helping to ward off the possibility of turning to antisocial groups as a way of belonging. Indeed, research has shown that kids involved in organized sports are often significantly less likely to become involved in antisocial activities. Quite a few professional athletes have credited organized sports for keeping them off the streets and out of potential trouble.

As parents, we can never start too early to try to develop a team concept with our kids in sports. Dr. Thomas Tutko, a sports psychologist, points out that, in the early years (ages

6-8), it's a little tough to develop the idea of "we" instead of "me." In fact, most youngsters in that age range end up playing youth sports because their parents sign them up. Tutko points out that the "team" concept begins to develop during the ages nine to thirteen. Many of the kids in this age range are playing a particular sport because their "buddies" are playing.

My youngest son, Matt, at age nine, made a choice to play Spring soccer instead of the traditional Spring Little League baseball. He and his "buddies" had been playing soccer during the previous Fall season, and they had continued to play soccer on the school grounds during the winter at recess. Since most of his buddies chose to play "Select" soccer in the Spring, he opted to go with them, drawn by the strong sense of belonging. The following year he returned to baseball, having met some new "buddies" who were into baseball. Interestingly, he "substituted" on the soccer team during the Spring when it didn't interfere with his baseball schedule. He was still drawn to his old "buddies."

Developing A Team Concept

I mention all this to point out that, as parents, we can go a long way in helping our kids develop the feeling of belonging on a team if we emphasize the team concept. The earlier we start developing the team concept, the better. We may not get as big of a response during those earlier years, but as the later years develop, the kids will really respond to feeling like they belong to a team.

There are lots of ways that parents can contribute to developing a team atmosphere for their kids.

Getting to know all the kids on the team and their parents is a good start. The coach usually calls a "team meeting" at the beginning of the season. Attending the meeting and offering support is a good start. Granted, not all parents have schedules which allow them to make all meetings, or even all the games. And, granted, not all parents have the same personalities or beliefs. But, a show of "togetherness" is a good beginning for developing a team spirit.

If parents get to know all the kids on the team, they can compliment each kid individually at games or practice, or they can say hello when they see a kid in the community. It may seem like it's a small token, but, as the quote at the beginning of the chapter indicates, kids often feel special when other parents know them and recognize them as part of the team.

The *team mom* (or *dad*) can be very instrumental in promoting the team concept, putting together the team roster with names, phone numbers, and addresses of all the kids and their parents; spreading the "snacks" assignments to all the parents; helping to get the parents involved in the team banner, and organizing the many other activities that help everyone get to know each other and support the team.

Team parties during the season can be very helpful in getting kids to think in terms of "we" instead of "me."

At the games, parents can promote team identity by complimenting all the kids on the team, not just the "super stars." **The Positive Behavior Checklists** in the Appendix once again offer lots of specifics for recognizing any kid on the team. Even the kid who hardly ever gets in the game can be complimented for cheering the team on. We shouldn't hesitate to yell out a compliment. Kids love to hear cheers. I saw one parent using a megaphone to yell out positive remarks to individual players. It was very effective.

A word of caution: please be careful not to complain publicly about "weak" players on the team. The movie *Parenthood*, in which Steve Martin played a Little League coach whose son was the weakest player on the team, portrayed parents and kids who kept complaining, in front of the kid, that he shouldn't be playing! Bickering, and backstabbing by parents can destroy team spirit in a heartbeat. In addition, parents shouldn't let their kids put down any of the players on the team. Remember, we're role models, and it's hard for a kid to remain silent when parents are ranting and raving about a kid on the team who is "pulling everybody down."

Nicknames are a great team identity builder. I remember one year, when my oldest son, Tom, was in the 6th grade. His baseball coach gave him the nickname of "Top Gun" because, as a catcher, he had a strong throwing arm. When I went to his games, I heard the parents and teammates cheering for "Top Gun." He was beaming, and the team spirit was obvious. Nicknames pull everyone together, but remember to keep the nicknames positive.

Showing lots of enthusiasm and forming a *parent cheering section* helps to continue the team feeling. I've seen parents form a "tunnel" for the team to run through at the beginning and end of a game. The kids loved it!

Coaches can obviously help tremendously in developing team spirit. Selecting different captains for each game allows every kid the opportunity to represent his/her team during the season. Individual awards at the end of the season, recognizing each individual kid for individual achievement, really promote a feeling of team membership and belonging. One team used the **Positive Behavior Checklists** in the Appendix for specific awards for each member of the team. No one was left out, regardless of skills.

Teamwork and team identity are major components of youth sports. They help build a sense of belonging. And, sometimes, lifetime friendships are developed among kids and parents alike, from the team experiences in youth sports. It would be a shame to waste the opportunity. Remember, if your kid is in youth sports, so are you! Anything you can do to promote the team concept will be energy well spent!

V. Step Into Their Shoes

"How would I feel as a child, if I had just been told what I said to my kid?" — Empathy exercise for adults

Empathy: Seeing Youth Sports Through the Eyes of Our Kids

Two of the cornerstones of self esteem are a sense of belonging and a sense of dignity. It is very difficult for children to feel worthwhile or respected if the adults in their world don't seem to want to take the time to see the world through the eyes of a child.

The World According to the Youth Leaguer

When it comes to youth sports, we run the risk of forgetting what it's like in the "world according to the youth leaguer." We sometimes forget that our kids are just kids, and not small adults. Sometimes, as parents, we get so wrapped up in the youth sports experience that we lose sight of what it's all about. I heard a dad yelling at his eight year old boy during the fourth quarter of a soccer game. He yelled out, "This is the fourth quarter! This isn't time to let up. You've gotta turn it up a notch!" The kid became tearful, upset that his dad was doubting that he was giving it his all. In fact, the little guy was exhausted. The game had mistakenly been scheduled on the adult soccer field, and the boy had been running, non-stop, during the previous three quarters. Dad had not arrived until the end of the third quarter. After the game, I heard the coach talking to the dad, reminding him not to ask his kid to do anything he couldn't do himself. In other words, running up and down that large soccer field was more than dad, or most adults, could have done for four quarters. In reality, the coach was asking the dad to have some **empathy** for his kid.

Non-Verbal Messages

As the quote at the beginning of the chapter reminds us, we have to be aware of the feelings we may generate in our kids through our communications to them. As adults, it's important for us to pay attention to *how we come across* in our communications, verbal and non-verbal, with our kids. Our non-verbal communication, for example, can have quite an effect on our kids. If we act bored while our kids are trying to tell us something, this conveys the message that the kids are not worth our time. If we use an intimidating tone of voice, this alone can make kids feel that they are not respected.

Comparisons

In our verbal communications, statements of comparison can be devastating to our kids. Simple remarks about siblings or even about our own experiences can convey to our kids that they somehow don't meet our approval. I heard a mother say to her 10 year old soccer playing son, "Your older brother played goalie when he was 10, and he didn't need goalie gloves to hold on to the ball!" I heard a dad say to his 11 year old son, who had just struck out on a curveball, "One of the first things I learned as an 11 year old was how to hit a curveball." I heard another dad comparing his 12 year old basketball playing daughter to her older sister, who had been selected to an "all city" team at age 13, "You've got to be able to go to your left! Your sister was going to her left when she was 11!" Comparisons simply wear away at self esteem.

Listening

Another essential part of communication is listening. We have to remember to listen to our kids, using eye contact, and a tender touch while they talk about the many disappointments and/or fears connected with youth sports. Listen, while our kids tell us about not getting chosen for the position they wanted. Listen, while they tell us their disappointment at being on a team with none of their friends. Listen, while they talk about being afraid of getting hit by the ball. Listen, while they talk about being afraid to make a mistake on the field or court. We don't have to have all the answers. Many times the problems solve themselves. But kids need to feel that their parents understand that they're *just kids*. In my parenting workshops, listening is often the number one issue between kids and their parents.

Youth Sports Survey: Fun is Number One

Do you want to know what your kids' world is like when it comes to youth sports? Some recent surveys may shed some light.

In 1990, the Athletic Footwear Association, as quoted by Amy Gibbons in "Why do Kids Play Sports?" in *Sportscene,* surveyed over 20,000 youth on their outlook about sports and why they do or do not participate. According to this study, the ten most important motives on why kids play sports are the following:

1. To have fun

2. To improve their skills

3. To stay in shape

4. To do something they are good at

5. For the excitement of competition

6. To get exercise

7. To play as part of a team

8. For the challenge of the competition

9. To learn new skills

10. To win

In addition, the study concluded that over 65% of kids participate in sports because they want to be with their friends. Approximately 15% are reluctant participants, and only 20% are active participants who truly want to improve their skills. I mention this study to remind us, as parents, that winning is at the bottom of the list for most kids who play youth sports. Need more evidence? A recent survey by the UCLA Sports Psychology Laboratory found the same results.

Process vs. End Product

There's another thing to remember in the world of youth sports, especially in the earlier years. As Dr. Tutko notes, kids are more concerned with the process of play than they are with the end product. Adults are preoccupied with the

Dad consoling his son after the game

end product, with questions like "Who won?", or "Who scored?" Kids are interested in questions like "Who was there?" "Was it fun?" "Were the uniforms cool?" or "How were the snacks?" Indeed, to paraphrase a recent tv commercial, for kids, sometimes the most important question is not about winning or losing, but about where everybody's going to eat after the game!

Youth Sports: It's All About Being a Kid

I heard two kids talking one day. They summed up the two extremes at the opposite ends of the spectrum of parental empathy:

One boy said, "My mom is cool. She watches, she cheers, and she listens when I've got problems. She still remembers what it's like to be a kid."

The other boy said, "You're lucky. My dad just lectures. He gets me all the really good equipment, but he hardly ever comes to my games. I'm afraid to tell him I don't like sports that much. He wouldn't understand."

Some parents have trouble remembering what it was like to be a kid. Perhaps it was too painful. If our kids are in youth sports, and if we really want to help make it a positive experience, we've got to make the effort to let our kids be kids, and to remember to see youth sports through the eyes of our youth leaguers. We've got to remember what youth sports is all about. It's not all about winning and losing and standings. It's all about *kids*. It's all about kids who are learning to play with other kids. It's all about kids who are learning to have fun, to take turns, and to learn new skills. And it's also about kids learning to handle defeat, mistakes, pain, fear, and disappointment, buoyed up by empathic parents.

VI. Involve Yourself

"We have a few special years with our children when they're the ones that want us around. After that, you're going to be running after them for attention. It goes so fast. It's just a few years. Then it's over."

— Peter Pan's wife to Peter in the movie *Hook*

Parental Involvement:
Making Our Kids Feel Important

Did you ever notice what happens on the typical vacation with the kids? You find a place with a pool. You sit down under the umbrella, relaxing poolside. The kids get in the water. And then it begins: the repeated chanting of those same two words, over, and over, and over. They yell out to you, "Watch me!" "Watch me!" "Watch me!" They do spins and jumps and dives, and with each spin, jump or dive, they yell, "Watch me!" It's as though the spin, jump, or dive doesn't count unless you see it!

Why do kids do this? I think part of the reason is the basic need to belong, which we described earlier, and the need to feel *worthwhile*. The kid's reasoning goes something like this, "If Mom or Dad take the time to watch me do my thing, they must think I'm pretty important. If they're more involved in something else (reading the newspaper, talking on the phone, or working), then I guess I'm not that important to them." This logic may be wrong, it may be very self-centered, but, in the mind of a kid, especially at the earlier ages, it makes perfect sense.

Parental Involvement: Find a Way

We, as parents, should make every effort to set aside the time to involve ourselves in our kids' youth sports activities. Our involvement will enhance our children's participation. Besides the obvious volunteer tasks (coaching, lining the fields, keeping score, sponsoring, helping at the snack bar, and helping with publicity), there are other, more subtle ways of being involved: *asking* our kids about what they learned at practice, asking about the other players on the team, asking about the coaches, or *listening* (with eye contact) while our kids talk about practice, the other players, or the coach. *Practicing* at home with your kids as they work on basic skills is always helpful, and it makes them feel that you're involved. **The Skills Checklists** in the Appendix offers lots of areas for practice. If you are repeatedly "too busy" when your kids ask to toss, shoot, throw, or kick the ball in the back yard, you're sending a message to your kids about how much you care about their involvement in the sport.

I can remember an incident with my youngest son, Matt. He had just started playing T-Ball and Coach-Pitch baseball. My mother was visiting with us in California during the cold winter months. The warm sunshine helped relieve her painful arthritis. One day, when I came home from work, I looked in the back yard. There was my mom, 75 years of age, with arthritic hands, tossing a wiffle ball underhanded to my son, age six, who was proudly swatting the ball with his oversized bat. He was having the time of his life showing his grandma that he could hit the ball! I was so taken by the scene that I videotaped it. As my son grows older, he likes to get out the tape to remember the joy his grandma brought him before she died at age 78, just by taking the time to practice with him, painful hands and all.

Youth Sports as a "Baby Sitting" Service

It's understandable that parents can't devote every waking moment to be involved with their kids in sports. Unfortunately, I've seen cases where there is little or no involvement. I have seen situations in which the parents used youth sports as a "baby sitting" service. They simply drop the kid off at practice or the game (sometimes without the necessary sports equipment) and come back afterwards. In one of my own situations, a mother of one of the kids on the team I was coaching asked me to take her kid home afterwards because she was going shopping and then out to a movie! The kid was forever making excuses for his parents' lack of involvement all season. Whenever he made a good play, I knew he was aching because there was no one from his family to watch him!

Parental Involvement: Seize the Opportunity

The quote from the movie *Hook* at the beginning of the chapter makes a good point. In the movie, Peter Pan is an adult with kids of his own. One of them is a Little Leaguer. Peter's work schedule is very demanding, so he seldom comes to his son's games. On this occasion, he misses a game which he had promised he would attend. His wife reminds him that there are certain years when kids *want* their parents' involvement (usually the early years up until the teens), and those are the years when it is important for parents to make time in their busy schedules to be with their kids. When those years are gone, the shoe will be on the other foot. The parents will want their kids' involvement, but the kids, growing up, will be too busy. The late Harry Chapin described the same phenomenon is his song, "Cat's in the Cradle."

The youth sports years are the golden years for family involvement. We're living in an age where it is estimated that dads spend less than 20 minutes a day with their kids. Never underestimate the value of your involvement. It means so much to your kid! One time, just before a basketball game, a ten year old boy was scanning the stands looking for his dad. I overheard him say, "I hope Dad comes. I've been working on a new move, and I want to show him what I've got!" Dad showed, and the kid beamed. Another game, another golden opportunity for parental involvement and enhanced self esteem.

The games, the practices, the team picnics, the team banquets, all offer time for involvement with our kids, giving them the assurance that they are important, and that sports activities are not just a convenient baby sitter.

Over-involvement

One word of caution: there is sometimes a danger of *too much* involvement.

It doesn't happen often, but it can happen. Too much involvement is sometimes an embarrassment for a youth leaguer. I've seen parents become obsessed with youth sports to the point of making the rest of their family life take backstage. I've seen parents totally preoccupied with "their kid, the athlete." I've seen parents become so involved that they begin challenging the coach's decision about how often, and which position their kid should play. There was one mother who removed her son from a soccer team because she felt he was being "wasted" at fullback position. She saw him as a natural forward. The boy was eight years old! Then there was a dad who protested to the league because it was using rubberized baseballs for safety. Dad said it was not preparing his son for "real" baseball. The boy was six years old!

VII. Notice Any & All Progress

"The smallest progress is still progress!"

Seeing Progress in Skill Development: A Feeling of Control

In the first chapter we noted that a sense of control is one of the four cornerstones of self esteem. The extent to which people feel in control of their environment has a definite effect on their self confidence.

In youth sports, one of the ways to help kids develop self confidence is to help them develop *skills* in a sport. The skills are in three areas: eye-hand **coordination**, use of the **tools** of the sport (ball, bat, glove, and other equipment), and knowledge of the **rules** of the sport. The more youth leaguers develop these skills, the more in control they feel. The more they feel in control, the less fear they have, the more confidence they have, and the more they can enjoy the sport and have fun.

Remember what we said about self esteem and self confidence in Chapter I? Kids develop their view of themselves based upon what they hear about themselves from others. So, if we want our kids to see themselves as in control in a given sport, it well help if they hear from us that they are making progress in the three skill areas listed above (eye-hand coordination, use of the tools of the sport, and knowledge of the rules).

In the early years, if kids see themselves as not doing well in sports, they may give up easily, stop trying, and eventually quit the sport. However, if they see *progress*, any kind of progress, no matter how small, they may stay with it long enough to the point of developing the skills necessary to really enjoy the sport, and to enjoy the feeling of self confidence that comes from feeling "in control" on the field or court.

As parents we can help our kids notice some progress in themselves at every practice and every game. We can call their attention to their progress, and we can get them to notice and keep track of their own progress.

Unfortunately, as we mentioned in Chapter II, lots of kids tend to focus on their *failures*, rather than their successes. They seem to be preoccupied with comparing themselves to other kids whom they think are "better" than they are. They yell at themselves for their mistakes, while they ignore their successes, or take them for granted. That's why we, as parents, have to make sure that we concentrate on every small step of progress with our kids, getting them to do the same. We have to get our kids to *compete against themselves*, noting areas of progress, rather than comparing themselves to how others are doing in a given sport.

Measuring Progress

When you think about it, there's always some kind of progress we can get kids to notice in themselves as they participate in sports.

There are three main areas we can look at when we're looking for progress. Simply defined, progress is movement toward a goal. This means any movement, toward any goal! And that movement can be measured in three areas:

1. **Frequency** (How OFTEN something happens.)
2. **Duration** (How LONG something lasts.)
3. **Intensity** (How much ENERGY is involved.)

Using the **Skills Checklists** and the **Positive Behavior Checklists** in the Appendix, for example, we, as parents can help our kids concentrate on their progress in all the items on the Checklists, in the areas of frequency, duration, and intensity. At the end of this chapter, I have put together some sample **Progress Charts**, using a few items from the Checklists in the Appendix. Each chart gives a few examples for each sport. The charts are just samples, meant to give you an idea of how we can focus on progress in our kids. With a little creativity, we parents can expand the charts for each sport, helping to keep the focus on progress, rather than failure. Let's take a look at the three areas of frequency, duration, and intensity.

Frequency

Frequency can focus either on how often a *desired* behavior occurs, or how infrequently an *undesired* behavior occurs.

You will notice from the progress charts that progress can be in very basic areas. For example, an eight year old Little Leaguer may overthrow the ball to second base on a forceout. Instead of criticism for the overthrow, there should be some attention paid to the fact that the kid threw to the correct base! That's progress!

Don't underestimate what it can mean to kids when they are able to see progress in even the smallest area. In baseball, for example, being able to "contact the ball with the bat" may seem elementary. But, if a kid is struggling with eye-hand coordination, or if a kid is up against a "super star" pitcher, just contacting the ball can be progress. I have the privilege of coaching developmentally delayed youngsters in the Challenger Division of Little League. Last season, at the beginning of the season, most of the kids began hitting off the batting tee. Toward the end of the season they were all hitting pitched balls! Talk about a feeling of progress, a sense of pride, and a sense of control! One of our kids on the team has C.H.A.R.G.E. syndrome. Some of his organs are on the opposite side of his body. He also has some severe vision alignment problems, with one eye socket lower than the other. He insisted on trying to hit the pitched ball rather than hit it off the tee. He started off measuring his progress by just touching the ball. By the end of the season he was consistently putting the ball in play . He kept trying because he kept seeing progress. On another occasion, at a AAA level game, I saw a nine year old take pride in being able to make contact against a pitcher who had struck him out two times previously. He grounded to first. But, as he came back to the dugout, he yelled out to his parents that he "got a piece of it!" That's a kid who's going to keep trying, because he sees progress.

Likewise, helping a kid notice a decrease in the frequency of an undesired behavior can also be progress. In the example of the nine year old boy with the two strikeouts, he might be taught to notice progress if he lowers his strikeouts to one in the next game.

Notice from the progress charts that the behavior being noted may have nothing to do with a specific athletic skill. One of the behaviors noted in the progress chart has to do with temper tantrums. Thus, for some youngsters, progress may be their ability to "keep their cool", cutting down the number of times they scream, push, or blame others when things aren't going well for them in the game or on the sidelines.

Duration

Sometimes we become so preoccupied with how often something happens or doesn't happen that we fail to notice progress in another area, namely, *how long* something lasts or doesn't last. In order to make sure we notice progress in every area possible, it helps to keep progress charts which measure how long a desired behavior lasts, or how short an undesired behavior lasts.

Being able to do something for an extended period of time gives kids a feeling of progress. Instead of allowing a kid to focus on a missed foul shot in basketball, for example, as we discussed in Chapter I, with the dad who yelled at his boy whose missed foul shot led to overtime, the focus should have been on the consecutive successful foul shots. In the example cited, the boy had actually made four foul shots in a row before missing the fifth one. The dad should have reminded his son that, had he not made the four consecutive foul shots, they wouldn't even have been able to get to the overtime! Likewise, in football, if a quarterback is focussing on an incomplete pass on third down, it may help to focus on the consecutive complete passes he may have had prior to the incompletion.

Remember also to help a youngster measure progress in terms of a shorter duration of an undesired behavior. In the example of the pouting baseball player, progress could be measured by shortening the duration of the pout! A young shortstop who stops pouting after an error, and pulls it together before the next batter comes up, is making progress! Notice it, and praise it!

Intensity

Once again, since we want to try to notice progress in as many areas as we can, we have to remember not to get so preoccupied with frequency or duration that we forget another important area of progress: intensity. This is an area often overlooked as a source of praise for a youth leaguer, and yet this is an area that kids can excel in, regardless of athletic ability. This is the area of *desire and energy.* There are kids who may not be the most gifted athletes on the team, but their intensity may spark the other kids to hustle and to use their skills to the best of their ability. This is worth noting! The kids with all out effort deserve to be noticed as much as the kids with more tackles, goals, and hits. I have often seen coaches give out awards after games for the most outstanding play of the game, or most hits, tackles, or goals. Every once in a while I have seen coaches give awards for "hustle", but not as often as the other awards. There are lots of ways to help our kids see progress, if only in their effort and energy. We've got to remember to notice the kids who hustle on the field, who run full speed , who play out every minute of the game, or who stay in a play until the whistle blows. We've got to notice those kids, praise those kids, and make sure those kids realize the progress they're making just by giving it their all during a game or practice.

In summary, then, if we can get our kids to keep track of their progress in the areas of frequency, duration, and intensity , we'll be helping them see how they're gradually gaining control over the sport they're playing, and this will add to their enjoyment and confidence. One final word. It's also a great idea to get kids to focus on the progress of their teammates. This really helps develop the team concept. Instead of putting a teammate down, kids can be asked to notice some progress a teammate is making (making more contact at the plate, dribbling with both hands, staying in position on the soccer field longer, or hustling on and off the field more). I've seen some coaches in their post-game wrap up with the kids, get them to notice progress in each team member for that day. I've also seen parents notice progress in other kids on the team, regardless of the score or outcome of the game. With our kids in the Challenger Division of the Little League, each kid gets a baseball card after each game, noting a special area of progress. The kids applaud each other. They love it!

Progress Chart I: Frequency

Instructions: Keep a record of how *often* a"desired" skill or behavior occurs.

Baseball/Softball

__ Contacting the ball with the bat
__ Getting in front of grounders
__ Throwing to the correct base
__ Running out a grounder

Basketball

__ Passing and getting assists
__ Getting back on defense
__ Blocking out on defense
__ Moving without the ball

Football

__ Getting first downs
__ Blocking
__ Completing Passes
__ Running "tight" pass patterns

Soccer

__ Passing
__ Going to the ball
__ Shooting on goal
__ Throwing-in correctly

Progress Chart II: Frequency

Instructions: Keep a record of how *seldom* an "undesired" skill or behavior occurs.

Baseball/Softball

__ Making an error
__ Daydreaming
__ Throwing temper tantrums
__ Striking out

Basketball

__ Double dribbling
__ Walking with the ball
__ "Telegraphing" passes
__ Shooting "air balls"

Football

__ Being offsides
__ Holding
__ Fumbling
__ Missing a tackle

Soccer

__ Being offsides
__ Criticizing a teammate
__ Being out of position
__ Daydreaming

Progress Chart III: Duration

Instructions: Keep a record of how *long* a desired behavior lasts or how *short* an undesired behavior lasts.

Baseball/Softball
__ Three innings without an error
__ "Chattering" for an entire inning
__ No "dandelion picking" for an entire inning
__ Stopping a "pout" after an error, before the next batter gets up

Basketball
__ Making three foul shots in a row
__ Passing to open teammates three times in a row
__ Going a whole quarter without a turnover
__ Hustling for an entire half

Football
__ Going one quarter without a turnover
__ Blocking correctly on three consecutive plays
__ Going an entire half without a turnover
__ Completing three passes in a row

Soccer
__ Going one quarter without an offsides
__ Blocking three consecutive shots on goal
__ Having three consecutive correct throw-ins
__ Hustling to the ball for one entire quarter

Progress Chart IV: Intensity

Instructions: Keep a record of the *energy* and *effort* put forth by a player.

Baseball/Softball

__ Running out all hits at full speed
__ Taking a full swing when at bat
__ Hustling to a ball in the gap
__ Hustling on to the field and off

Basketball

__ Going full speed to get back on defense
__ Diving for a loose ball
__ Moving quickly without the ball
__ Playing "all-out" every minute of the game

Football

__ Making a second effort on a tackle
__ Hustling for a fumble
__ Carrying out a fake
__ Staying in a play until the whistle blows

Soccer

__ Hustling to keep the ball in bounds
__ Hustling to make a quick throw-in
__ Hustling downfield to cut off an opponent
__ Hustling to an open ball

VIII. Show Excitement & Enthusiastic Praise

"I don't get it! My parents yell and scream when I screw up. But when I get it right, they act like they expect it!"

— Frustrated ten year old

Enthusiastic Praise and Calm Correction

Chapter II discussed the importance of noticing positives in our kids. Chapter VII discussed the many ways of noticing positive progress in our kids. Now we need to talk about how to respond to the positives, and how to offer correction to our kids. It was mentioned in Chapter II that we should try to keep the ratio of four to one when it comes to encouragement versus correction. This frequency ratio is important, but we also have to pay attention to the *way* we encourage and correct.

Action, Commotion, & Emotion

In general, we should be **enthusiastic** in our encouragement, and **calm** in our correction. Why? In the movie *Pretty Woman*, a man befriends a call girl. As they talk, she relates her life as a child, noting that she grew up hearing a lot of negatives about herself. She notes that, after hearing enough negatives about herself she began to believe them. The man asks her if she ever heard anything positive about herself when she was growing up. She says that the negatives are what she remembers.

When I heard that line in the movie I began to think about why that's true for a lot of people. I began to think about why people often tend to remember the negatives that have been said to them, especially when they were children. I think I understand why. I think it's because when we're kids, we're tuned into action. Someone once said that, for kids, "action is the attraction." So, when kids get a response from an adult that's full of *action, commotion, and emotion*, that's what they pay attention to, and that's what they remember. Why do we remember the negatives from childhood? Think about it. When is it that adults show action, commotion, and emotion to their kids? Is it when the kids are being "good," doing what adults want them to do? Or, is it when they're being "bad," doing something adults don't want them to do? Odds are, in the average family, if dad comes home from work and his two kids are sitting quietly, doing their homework, dad casually says hello and goes about his business, with very little comment. However, if dad comes home and walks into the middle of an argument between the two kids, what's his response? In the most typical scenario, he gets upset and yells, with the veins bulging in his neck, something like, "I can't believe it! I've been in traffic for almost an hour. I walk in here, and all I get is more noise! I'm sick and tired of it! All I want is a little peace and quiet. Is that too much to ask? Can't you kids get along for one lousy hour? Go to your rooms!" So, when it comes to remembering childhood incidents, those two kids are more likely to remember their dad's reaction to their fight than his reaction to their studying.

The simple fact is that kids like action. They always have, and they always will. They like attention with lots of action. It may be hard to imagine, but kids often prefer negative attention to no attention at all. So, if we want our kids to get our attention for positive behaviors, we have to make sure that our attention for positive behaviors is full of action, commotion, and emotion. If they show undesired behaviors and we respond with calm correction rather than the yelling, screaming, and threatening that often accompany our responses to unwanted behaviors, the kids will be less likely to keep trying to get our attention with the undesired behaviors, and they won't have as many negative childhood memories.

The lesson is easily transferable to youth sports. Parents need to make a "big deal" when giving encouragement and praise for positives and progress, and they must try to be calm when correcting a mistake.

Encouragement and Correction: Some Examples

Here are some examples of how to correct mistakes **calmly** while **excitedly** encouraging progress in youth sports.

In baseball or softball, if your kid is having difficulty getting down on ground balls, instead of repeatedly yelling, "Get down on the ball! Get down on the ball!", you might take the kid aside after the game, excitedly talking about the kid's progress, and calmly give some instruction on how to field the ball with the glove near the ground. The conversation might go something like this: "That's the way to hustle over to get in front of that ball! You're really getting better at moving quickly to the ball. You're also bending down a little more on the grounders. I think you'll find it a little easier if you put your glove almost on the ground   and bend your knees, like this. We'll work at it in practice this week, ok? Keep up the hustle!" This approach, using Ned MacIntosh's "sandwich method" of criticism from his book, *Managing Little League Baseball,* places a corrective remark between two compliments and encouraging remarks. A positive approach is much more likely to get the kid's attention than a public scolding. Incidentally, it is always to good to remember the basic rule: **praise in public, criticize in private.**

In soccer, if your kid is having trouble with throw-ins, instead of repeatedly yelling, "Throw it over your head, not sidearm!" you might take your kid aside after the game, excitedly talking about progress and calmly giving advice, and say something like this: "I like the way you're keeping both feet on the ground during your throw-ins. You're getting better at throwing it overhead. I know it's tough. There are a few tricks to making sure it goes overhead each time. We can practice throw-ins this week at practice. By the way, you hit the open man perfectly on that last throw-in. Keep it up!" Once again, a calm remark coupled with excited compliments is likely to be heard by the kid. The enthusiastic positive remarks strengthen the kid's ego so that the correction can be heard and the kid can respond to the correction without feeling like a failure.

In basketball, if your kid is having trouble keeping up with the opposing player on defense, instead of yelling, "Stay between your man and the basket! Stay between your man and the basket!" you might take the kid aside, and say, "That's the way to keep your hands up on defense! I like your sidestep move with your feet! I know it's hard to remember everything at once during the game, but you'll probably save some energy on defense if you try to remember to keep yourself between your man and the basket. Maybe we can practice some special drills at practice this week. I'll draw some diagrams and we'll run through it in slow motion. I really like your hustle out there!"

In football, if your kid tends to forget to tuck the ball in when running with it, instead of frantically yelling, "You've got to protect the ball! You've got to protect the ball!", you might try something like this: "I like the way you hit the hole quickly, and the way you follow your blockers. Did you notice how the defense is going for the ball? It'll be harder for them to punch it out of your arms if you tuck it in tight. See if you can concentrate on keeping it tight. We'll practice more this week. Keep up those high knee kicks through the line. You look great!"

As parents, we all have our own "style" when it comes to talking to our kids. These examples are simply offered as reminders of how to combine encouragement with correction.

Seeing Mistakes as "Stepping Stones"

Remember, we're trying to build positive memories for our kids in youth sports. We want them to look back on their youth sports days as confidence builders. If we remain calm when they make mistakes, and try to help them learn from them, they won't be as likely to grow up being afraid to make a mistake.

One characteristic of people with low self esteem is their tendency to be extremely cautious, and to be preoccupied with not making any mistakes. They see mistakes as failures, and they live in fear of making another mistake. As a result, they seldom try new things, and they lose their creativity.

To boost our kids' self esteem in youth sports, we have to make sure that they see mistakes as stepping stones for growth, rather than as examples of failure. They have to learn that it's ok to make a mistake. One way to help them in this area is to calmly discuss stories of great sports figures who also made mistakes, and overcame them. In baseball, it helps to remind kids that Babe Ruth, one of the greatest home run hitters of all times, was also very high on the all time strikeout list! In football, it helps to remind kids that Terry Bradshaw had a horrible rookie year at quarterback with the Pittsburgh Steelers, and people were questioning whether he was smart enough to be a professional quarterback. Then he went on to win four Super Bowls! In basketball, kids always get a kick out of hearing that Michael Jordan, superstar basketball player, was cut from his Junior High basketball team!

High five

Accepting Responsibility For Mistakes

How often do we see kids who are so afraid to make a mistake that they become preoccupied with making excuses for an error, a missed shot, or a missed tackle. The fact is, being able to accept a mistake and to learn from it, with no excuses, is a common characteristic in top athletes. Dr. James Loehr, a sports psychologist, studied athletes who were tops in their field. He was interested in the mental aspect of their performance. He found several common characteristics in the athletes, regardless of the sport. One of them was accepting responsibility for mistakes. In other words, the top athletes hold themselves *accountable* for their performance. If they make a mistake, they don't blame it on equipment, weather, or injuries. They simply accept the mistake, learn from it, and try not to repeat the same mistake again. Apparently, they have enough self confidence that they can handle their errors as part of a learning process.

This idea of accountability for our actions is an essential part of growing up, and it's tied in with self esteem and self confidence. If I see myself as in control of things, then that means that I make choices, with consequences. I have to learn to accept those consequences, pleasant or unpleasant. I can't run away from an unpleasant consequence, I simply have to learn from it. If, for example, as a Little Leaguer, I miss a sign from my third base coach because I'm not paying attention, I have to accept the consequence and learn not to repeat the mistake again, rather than blame the coach or the crowd noise. Teaching our kids to accept their mistakes is no easy task. Lets face it, kids tend to make excuses. Their egos are fragile. So, if we, as parents, are going to get them to accept their mistakes and learn from them, we must concentrate on building their self confidence so that they will not be traumatized by a mistake. To help build the kids' confidence, we must be careful not to put too much emphasis on what they did wrong. They're feeling bad enough as it is when they make a mistake. If everybody starts yelling at them, it simply makes things worse, and there's very little learning going on. So, as we noted in the beginning of the chapter, if kids are having difficulty performing the way we want, we've got to find something positive in the situation, no matter how small, and make a "big deal" out of it. This will relax the kids and help them see the mistake as a learning experience, rather than a proof of their failure.

A Personal Note

Let me close this chapter with a personal story. I grew up in Cincinnati, Ohio, in the 1940s and '50s. In the parochial school system, there were strong sports programs for all age groups. I decided to play "pee wee" football. The smallest and youngest kid on the team, I barely made the minimum weight of 70 pounds. The coach carried me on the team and kept me safely out of harm's way for most of the season. However, in one particular game, there were a few players missing. In order not to forfeit, the coach had to play me most of the game. He put me at safety on defense, figuring I would be out of most of the heavy hitting plays. Well, on the last play of the game, the halfback from the other team broke through our line, eluded our secondary and came straight at me! I remember peering through my helmet, which was too large and kept falling down over my eyes. As the runner approached me, I crouched down to try to get ready to tackle him. All I can remember as he got closer was that he had all kinds of hair on his legs! Here I was, barely 70 pounds, trying to tackle this big guy with hair on his legs! I reached out for his legs, and I held on for dear life as he proceeded to drag me with him down the field. I remember banging my helmet on the hard dirt of the infield of the combination baseball/football field as he carried me all the way into the end zone! As I lay there completely mortified by the experience, my coach, the other players, and my mom came running out to *congratulate* me! The coach talked about how I never gave up and how I didn't let the big guy scare me away from trying to tackle him. The bigger kids on our team laughed about seeing the little "70 pounder" holding on for dear life. They said I had "guts." My mom was proud that I didn't break any bones. There I was, lying on the ground trying to fight back tears because I had let the other team score, and they all came out to congratulate me on my gutsy effort. I still remember that incident from over 40 years ago, and, wouldn't you know it, I can't remember whether we won or lost! I guess that's what it's all about.

IX. Praise Specifics

"Praise the deed, not the child!"

In previous chapters we have talked about the importance of praising positives, noticing progress, and being enthusiastic in our praise. Now we need to talk about the importance of being specific in our praise.

Kids "Hear" Specific Praise

As you may recall from Chapter I, we pointed out that kids' views of themselves are based upon what they hear about themselves from others. So, if we want kids to feel good about themselves, it will help if they hear positives about themselves. However, if the praise is not specific it may not sink in. That is, kids may not hear positives which are too vague or general. If we say, "nice game!", we may not get their attention. It's too general, it's said all the time, and it really doesn't focus on the kids. But, saying, "I like the way you tagged up to score the go ahead run!" is likely to stick with them, because it conjures up a specific incident and a specific visualization which the kids can recall. They can see themselves tagging up and scoring. As we've said over and over so far, we're trying to build positive memories through youth sports. Memory is enhanced through specific visualization. Kids tend to remember specifics, and forget general statements.

Specific Praise is Less Likely to be "Screened Out"

As was also noted in Chapter I, kids tend to screen out what doesn't match their image of themselves. So, if youth leaguers have a negative self view, or lack confidence, they are liable to screen out positives, especially if the positives are vague or general. That's all the more reason for us, as parents, to be very specific with our praise, especially if our kids get "down" on themselves. Why? Because at the moment kids are down on themselves they tend to get into a negative self view, and they tend to screen out anything positive. If we say "nice game," they may be thinking, "They're saying that because they think they have to. They don't mean it. How can they say 'nice game' when I screwed up so much?" If we want to get through to our kids when they're into a negative self view, we've got to emphasize specifics, based on facts, which they can't ignore. It's easy for them to screen out statements like, "You did your best!" "You gave it your all!" "We'll get 'em next time!" However, it's not so easy for them to screen out statements like "That throw to the cutoff man in the third inning was a thing of beauty!" Granted, they may still minimize the praise, but at least it's something specific, and they'll have a hard time screening it out. In fact, after the game's over, and the negative memories fade, they may be able to recall your positive praise, and bask in the visualization of their perfect throw to the cutoff man!

Using Checklists

At any rate, if we concentrate on specifics with our praise, we'll get better results. As we mentioned in earlier chapters, the checklists in the Appendix offer lots of specifics. In a series of booklets I wrote on youth league positive coaching, I included these checklists. Coaches have reported that the parents of their kids find the checklists useful for picking specifics to praise for each sport. Whether it's the **Skills Checklist**, or the **Positive Behavior Checklist**, as we mentioned in an earlier chapter, they offer a good start for parents to look for and find positives to praise in their kids. One coach told me of a group of parents who had the checklists enlarged as a huge poster. They had the poster laminated and took it to the game, posting it for all parents to see. The parents then cheered the kids on, recognizing the various specific positives on the list as they occurred. The coach said the kids really loved it when they heard parents yelling out the positives, "Way to go Billy, that's the way to pass to the open man!" "Johnny, way to hustle after that loose ball!" or "Mary, what a great throw-in!"

How do you rate as a praise giver? Do you get specific? It's really quite simple. Using the checklists in the Appendix, see how many specifics you already use.Think about all the times you've used "nice try" or "good game," and try to replace them with some "meaty" remarks.

Vague Versus Specific Praise: A Few Samples

Here are a few samples contrasting vague versus specific praise, taking some items from the checklists in the Appendix. Just for the fun of it, you might want to try this exercise. Go down the list of each item on the checklists and write examples of "vague vs. specific" praise for each item. It will get you into the habit of shouting out specifics at the games.

Vague: "Johnny, you're a good sport!"

Specific: "Johnny, I liked the way you shook their hands after the game, and didn't say anything mean."

Vague: "Johnny, you played good defense!"

Specific: "Johnny, you stayed on your man, and you switched off well on those picks!"

Vague: "Mary, good game!"

Specific: "Mary, you've really got those throw-ins down perfect!"

Vague: "Mary, you're a good team player!"

Specific: "Mary, I really liked how you found the open teammates with your passes!"

Vague: "Carlos, I like your enthusiasm!"

Specific: "Carlos, the way you hustle onto the field and off shows me a lot!"

Vague: "Carlos, you really kept your cool today!"

Specific: "Carlos, I like the way you didn't throw your bat or your helmet after that third strike."

Remember, when the kids hear specifics, there's a better chance that they'll remember them, pay attention to them, and believe them.

Praise The Deed, Not The Child

One word of caution. The quote at the beginning of the chapter encourages us to praise the deed, not the person. There is a reason for this. As you will recall from Chapter I, it was noted that it is important for kids' self esteem that they feel worthwhile, just as a person, not solely because of their looks, talents, or skills. If kids are called "good kids" or "bad kids" based on their *performance*, they may quickly begin to judge themselves and label themselves as "good" or "bad" based on their performance. So, it is very important, that, while we praise the deeds, performances, or efforts of our youth leaguers, we need to stress to them that they are "good" kids who are "loved", *regardless* of the presence or absence of athletic skills. While it is important to praise specific skills or actions with our kids, we don't want them to think of themselves as "good" or "bad" based on the presence or absence of their athletic skills. We have to watch out, within our family, lest kids judge themselves solely on their athletic prowess. As I mentioned in an earlier chapter, I have seen several high school athletes in my office who, after an injury ended their athletic career, became despondent because they felt they were worthless. Somewhere along the line they judged themselves and their worth solely on their skills in sports. As parents, we must do all that we can to make sure that our kids see themselves beyond the spotlight of the sports arena. It's never too early to start.

QUALITY TIME   Gail Machlis

(The "Quality Time" cartoon by Gail Macklis is reprinted with the permission of Chronicle Features, San Francisco, CA.)

X. Offer a Good Example

"What we desire our children to become, we must endeavor to be before them."

— Andrew Combe

Parents as Models

Like it or not, our kids look to us, especially in the earlier years, as models of how to act. If we're trying to get our kids to feel good about themselves and to show good sportsmanship in youth sports, we have to check our own behavior. How are we coming across to our kids? Do we show that we have a sense of positive self regard about ourselves? Do we show them that we are good sports at the games?

We said earlier that we have to help our kids not take themselves too seriously in the world of youth sports. How about us, as parents? Do we take youth sports too seriously?

We want our kids to learn from their mistakes. How do we handle our own mistakes? Can we admit to our kids that we make mistakes? I've seen lots of parents who simply have to "look good" in front of their kids, no matter what. Kids are watching us. They want to see what happens if we make a mistake. They want to see if we can admit to it, and learn from it. If we can't, we can hardly expect our kids to do so.

We want our kids to stay healthy, take care of their bodies, eat right, and exercise. How do we do, as parents, in these areas? You know the old saying: "I can't hear a word you're saying, your actions are drowning out all your words!"

Unsportsmanlike Conduct

Unsportsmanlike conduct by parents at youth league games is well documented in newspaper articles around the country. Bill Geist, a CBS News feature correspondent, in his book *Little League Confidential*, spells out scene after scene of overzealous parents who "lose it" at Little League games. On a radio sports talk show, I did a 15 minute telephone interview about the topic of "sports, kids, parents, and pressure." After the interview, the phone lines on the radio station were filled, for 90 minutes, with callers, many of whom were complaining about the unsportsmanlike conduct of the parents at the youth league games. Umpires called in, relating episodes of being threatened by parents over disputed calls. Coaches called in, citing incidents of parents using put-downs, sarcasm, and ridicule to try to "shake up" kids on the opposing team. Chet Forte, one of the talk show hosts, and former Director of "Monday Night Football" on ABC TV, cited an example of his own daughter, who, at age ten, was taunted relentlessly by adults from the opposing team to the point that she left the field in tears!

Why Parents "Lose It"

Fortunately, these parents are in the minority. But they get all the attention. There are several reasons offered for their behavior. Thomas S. Tutko, in his "Sports Psychology" newsletter, and Dan Sewell in the "Youth Sports Coach" newsletter, both make the same observation. They feel that the parents get too wrapped up in the competition of it all because they are living *vicariously* through their kid. In other words, if their kid makes an error, they feel it reflects on them. If their kid loses, they somehow feel that they lose.

Another explanation for parents who "lose it" at games comes from the research on self esteem, which indicates that people with low self image sometimes have a need to put others down in order to make themselves look good. Following this theory, it would seem that some parents have such a low self image that they have to put others down (coaches, officials, other kids) to make themselves, or their kid, look good.

Public versus Private Behavior

We have to be aware of our public behavior in youth sports. If we have a complaint about an official or a coach, we need to take it up with that person after the game, privately, and as adults. We must always remember that there is, indeed, life beyond youth sports. The father who feels that he has to publicly take a stand to show that he's backing his kid often makes things worse. Antagonistic remarks to officials, challenging remarks to coaches about play choice, player positions, and the like are simply interfering with the purpose of youth sports: having fun.

Not only are we not giving a good example when we "lose it" at a game or practice, but we're embarassing our kids, ruining their concentration, and taking away from the fun of the game.

Parents Confronting Parents

As parents, I think we have to group together on the positive side of sportsmanship, and confront the unsportsmanlike conduct in a parent or a coach. I know of one team where the coaches refused to "cheer" for the other team after a loss. The parents called a team meeting and reminded the coaches about being role models to their kids for sportsmanship. On another team, I saw one misguided parent, upset at the team's loss, jokingly lead the kids in a cheer for the other team: "2-4-6-8, who's the team we love to hate?" The other parents confronted her, and rightly so.

In yet another situation, a mother was apalled at the assistant coach on her eleven year old's football team. Her son was coming home in tears. Upon investigation she found out that the assistant coach, a volunteer parent, was repeatedly calling her son a "sissy," hitting him on his helmet and telling him to "get tough," pushing him physically against the wall, and telling him he needed to develop a "mean streak" if he wanted to play football. The assistant coach justified his actions as a way of "toughening up" the boy so he wouldn't get hurt. She relayed this to the head coach, who simply told her to "take it to the Board." She did, and both the assistant coach and the coach were reprimanded, and placed on probation.

I was umpiring the bases for a game of ten year old boys in Little League. It's amazing how much you hear from the stands when you're out on the field. A small group of parents from the home team were berating a boy at the plate from the visiting team who had gone hitless in two times at bat. As he came up the third time, the parents yelled out to their pitcher, "Here's an automatic out! He swings like a girl! He's afraid up there! Blow it by him!" I noticed the batter lower his head. He struck out a third time. The parents from the home team said to the pitcher as he came off the mound after the third out, "If they had more players like that kid, you'd have a no hitter!" The parents from the visiting team quickly sent the word back to the home team parents to stop their cruel remarks. They stopped, but the damage had been done.

The coach reminds the parents before the game to show good sportsmanship and to stay positive.

In some soccer tournaments, in an effort to keep parents positive, the sportsmanship award is tied in with *parental* behavior. Unfortunately, I've seen kids work their hardest to win the sportsmanship award, only to lose it because one parent gets carried away with emotion in the heat of the game, yelling critically at officials or coaches. In one tournament, I saw a coach and some parents remind a particular parent before the game to "keep her cool" or leave the stands.

Parents as Self Monitors

One final note: sometimes it's easier to spot "problems" in other parents and in coaches than it is to see our own actions. As parents, we need to hold a mirror up to ourselves, to see how we are coming across to our kids, to the other players, to the other parents, to the coaches, and to the officials. **The Parent Checklist** in the Appendix offers us a quick review of how we're doing in trying to promote self esteem in our kids through youth sports, including offering them a role model of sportsmanship and positive self esteem. If we see signs of poor sportsmanship, or if we get feedback from others that perhaps we're "losing it" at games or practice, we need to respond to that feedback, and put things in their proper perspective, once again reminding ourselves that we are models to our kids, and that there is *life beyond youth sports.*

XI. Remember to Have Fun

"The number one reason why kids participate in sports is **To have fun.***"*

> —Report from the 1990 Athletic Footwear Association survey of 20,000 kids on why they participate in sports

Fun is Number One

One day last season while I was coaching the developmentally challenged youngsters in the Challenger Division of Little League, I was enjoying the atmosphere. The kids were smiling, and giving each other "high fives." Parents were cheering them on. Laughter filled the field and the dugouts. As I was taking this all in, I looked across at another diamond, where the "non-challenged," non-developmentally delayed nine year olds were playing. The contrast was striking. A left fielder was crying, after dropping a fly ball. A parent was yelling at the umpire. The coach was yelling at his pitcher to "follow through" on his pitches. The atmosphere was tense.

I mention this to point out that the real purpose of youth sports is, above all, to **have fun**! What we were experiencing that day on our diamond is what youth sports is all about. The other diamond had somehow lost the "big picture" of fun and games.

As parents, we've got to remember to keep it fun for our kids. The fun times are what we want them to remember.

Interestingly, Dr. James Loehr, in studying top athletes, found that one of the common characteristics of peak performers in various sports was this: during their athletic performance, they were enjoying it and having fun! In Chapter III, we discussed how laughter and humor can enhance performance. Likewise, an atmosphere of fun helps kids learn better, relax, and do their best.

Fun and games make up the special world of kids. It's our job, as parents, to let them be kids when it comes to youth sports. I've seen well intentioned coaches of youth leaguers lose their team's attention during practice or a game because there was not an atmosphere of fun. No matter how skilled kids may be, boredom will quickly defuse their motivation to participate in sports. I know one youngster who quit baseball and moved over to soccer because he saw baseball as "boring". He said he had to stand around at practice, stand around in the field, and sit on the bench waiting to hit. He was having no fun, so he switched to soccer, where he said he at least could run around a lot. And yet, no sport has to be boring. There are lots of good training videos which show how to have action-packed, fun-filled practices, regardless of the sport. We'll talk more about this in the next chapter.

Fun: Take a Lesson from the Kids

As parents, we have repeated opportunities to help make youth sports fun for our kids. The best way is to get our kids to see youth sports not as a task, but as an activity, a fun process. In fact, we can take a lesson from our kids on how to have fun. At the earlier years, videotape youngsters throughout a game, and you'll probably see lots of evidence that they're having fun. See if any of these scenarios ring true.

— The tiny young goalie in soccer, who, bored because all the action is at the other end of the field, starts climbing the soccer net, pretending to be GI Joe in combat!

— The center fielder on the T-Ball team who, discovering a turtle in the outfield, signals her teammates, and play stops while they all check it out!

— The pee wee football player, back to receive a punt, who proudly waves to his mom in the snack bar, while the ball sails over his head!

— The tiny basketball player, with trunks reaching almost to his ankles, who, in the middle of a game, stops at mid-court to talk to his "buddy", who's playing on the court next to his.

— The kid who stops what he's doing and heads for the water when the sprinklers come on at a practice or game.

The examples are endless. These are the fun times, and, as parents, we have to be careful not to take them away by losing sight of what youth sports is all about. Sometimes, we tend to get too preoccupied with standings, playoffs, tournaments, all-star teams, etc., forgetting , as we noted in an earlier chapter, that our kids are into *process* more than

the *end product.* In fact, I've seen parents take losses harder than the kids, because the parents were more concerned with the end product. We'll talk more about this in Chapter XIII.

In Chapter V we talked about trying to get into the "World according to the youth leaguer." A kid's definition of fun varies from kid to kid. I remember asking my team of eight year olds in AA Little League how they were going to have fun in the game that day. Several kids mentioned the fun of hitting, fielding, running, etc.. But one of the kids said he was looking forward to "throwing the infield dirt up in the air and trying to balance it on his baseball cap!" To each his own!

And it's not just the little kids who are into fun. My 11 year old son was in a soccer tournament, out of town. While the games were intense, the kids were relaxed throughout the tournament, and one of the highlights was the "fun and games" in the pool at the local hotel where the kids and parents stayed. The good natured horseplay in the pool between the kids and dads contributed to a relaxed atmosphere throughout the tournament, which allowed the team to play their best. They won the tournament easily, their first and only tournament championship. And yet, a year later, they're still talking about the fun they had in the pool at the hotel. The first place ribbons are simply gathering dust, but the memories of fun linger on.

Anything we can do as parents to increase the "fun" will help. Practice games, with parents against kids, father-daughter games, mother-daughter games, mother-son games, practices, scrimmages, picnics, parties, etc., can all help remind us that:

After All is Said and Done,

Having Fun is Number One!

The "Not-So-Fun" Times

A word of caution. There will, inevitably, be some "not-so-fun" times. We can't avoid them. And, we can't always "rescue" our kids from unpleasant events. They're going to lose games. They're going to make errors. Helping them make it through the setbacks is just as important in developing self esteem, as celebrating victory with them. Sometimes it's awkward for us. We may not know what to say. Sometimes we may turn to old cliches to try to get our kids out of the doldrums, only to find that it doesn't work. I remember when my youngest son was 8 years old. He was pitching and getting clobbered by the other team, 12-1! I took him aside, and, in my best fatherly voice, said, "Matt, just remember, this is just for fun." He looked up at me and said, "Yeah, right, dad! Did you ever have fun when you were losing 12-1?" Ooops! I guess I would have been better off just being there for him, and not offering advice. In fact, sometimes we're better off as parents just letting our kids experience the sting of defeat. If we wait a while, it'll usually wear off, they'll be better for it, and then we can concentrate on putting the fun back in their life.

XII. Teach Skills

"Two of the top ten reasons kids participate in sports are: to learn new skills, and to improve their skills."

— Report from 1990 Athletic Footwear Association survey of 20,000 kids on why they participate in sports

Skills: A Sense of Control

One of the major cornerstones of self esteem is a sense of control. As we noted in Chapter VII, the more kids learn the skills necessary to perform and participate in a sport, the more the kids feel "in control". That's why we, as parents need to do what we can to teach our kids, as best we can, the basic skills for a sport. The coach will concentrate on basics, but the coach has only a limited amount of time to deal with so many kids on a team. The time that our kids practice at home with us can be time well spent. Remember, we're not preparing them for professional athletics at age seven, we're just giving them an opportunity to practice what they're learning from their coach, and to help them begin to feel comfortable in their sport. They can sometimes be more relaxed at home, and this often enhances their ability to learn a new skill.

Practice, Practice, Practice

They say that "practice makes perfect," but that's only true if you're practicing the skill correctly. So, as parents, we've got to try to make sure that we're helping our kid practice the *correct* skill.

What's a parent to do? We're not all former athletes. How can we be sure we're practicing the correct skill for the sport? Usually, if you go to a practice, you'll see what the coach is working on with the kid. If you talk to the coach, you'll get some helpful hints. The **Skills Checklist** in the Appendix lists some basic skills which you can work on with your kid.

Fortunately, there are some excellent video training films on teaching basic skills, including the ESPN Youth Coaching Series, The Major League Baseball Coaching Clinic video, "Your Best Shot," a basketball shooting clinic video, or any of the video training films offered by the national organizations of youth sports. (For a more complete list of reference materials, please see the reference section in the back of the book.)

Teaching A Skill: Make It Relevant

There are lots of ways to teach skills to our kids, but the best way is to use live examples from their lives, or examples with which they can identify. When they come home from practice, ask them, "What did you learn today?" If you take them to a high school, college or professional game, point out to them a specific skill which a player has (batting stance of a baseball player, "soft hands" of a wide receiver in football, a basketball player who moves well without the ball, a soccer player who kicks with both feet, etc.). Kids learn more quickly if something seems *relevant or immediate* to them.

I saw a great example of skill teaching when my eleven year old son went to a summer basketball camp. Randy Pfund, the coach of the Los Angeles Lakers , was guest coach for a day. He spent the day teaching the kids four basic skills to practice. For each of the four skills, he gave them an example of an NBA player who had that particular skill, and he recommended that they watch those four players on TV during the year, looking for the particular skill they were practicing. My son immediately connected the player with the skill. He started practicing the four skills the next day, imagining he was a particular NBA player. Now he's anxious to see the players in action on TV. Coach Pfund got my kid to practice a skill. My son has been to other camps, and they've taught skills, but this time the skills seem real and relevant.

Teaching a Skill: Fun and Success

If you're going to spend time practicing skills with your kids, make it fun, and make it full of successes. Kids, especially in the earlier years, learn from positive experiences. We talked about fun in the previous chapter. Without fun, kids get bored. Without success, they give up quickly. So, when you practice, make a game out of it, and start with a skill which the kid has already. At the beginning stages of baseball, for example, the oversized bat and ball make for immediate contact. The kid gets excited, and wants more. I've seen frustrated dads who go out in the back yard with their six year old and throw pitch after pitch after pitch, as the little guy misses the ball over, and over, and over. Start with the t-ball, and gradually work up to the thrown pitch. In basketball, start with the smaller balls, lower baskets, etc., and work up, rather than have the little kid heaving the huge ball toward a basket high above and getting frustrated. In soccer, don't expect a speedy dribbler, shooting with both feet from the start. In the next chapter we'll talk more about what we can realistically expect from our kids. Suffice it to say at this point that we can't expect young kids to practice, just for the sake of practicing. There has to be an element of fun, and the kids need to see progress and success.

Teaching A Skill: Starting too Early

This brings up another point. How old should our kids be before parents start to concentrate on teaching skills to our kids? Dr. Eric Margenau, sports psychologist, points out that many parents try to teach skills too early and end up getting frustrated, along with the kid. He relates his own experience with his four year old daughter. She asked to play tennis with him. He simply let her "play," no rules, no instruction on how to hold the racket. There were no "nos." The specifics of the game didn't matter, and when they finished he and she were both delighted to have played "tennis" together. He knew there would be plenty of time to add rules and instructions. We should take a lesson from this account. We have to beware of interfering with the fun of sports in those earliest of years, boring our youngsters with dull routine practices, lectures on rules, and frustration from practicing skills beyond their ability or level of coordination.

"Mental" Skills: Attitude and Effort

It is important to remember that skill in sports is not limited to the mechanics of eye-hand coordination. Attitude and effort also play a part in sports. As parents, we may not have a background in athletics, but we certainly have the creden-

tials to teach our kids about sportsmanship and the importance of "giving it our all" when we try something. That's
why the **Positive Behavior Checklists** emphasize attitude
and effort.

One of the attitude skills is how to handle mistakes. We
discussed this in Chapter VIII, but it bears repeating. As early
as possible, it is important that we teach our kids that, as Dr.
Margenau notes, if there is one truism in sports, it's that
winning isn't inevitable, but losing is. In baseball, for
example, a .300 batting average is considered a success. That
means that seven out of ten times a batter ends up losing.
Successful major league pitchers get knocked out of more
games than they finish. As we said before, we have to teach
our kids that it's *ok to make mistakes*. We can do our kids a
real favor if we teach them to "relabel" mistakes, so that they
can actually feel good about a mistake because it gives them
an opportunity to learn to do something the correct way.
Unfortunately, in many instances, kids label a mistake as
something "bad," and they feel bad about doing something
the wrong way. As parents, when our kids make a mistake,
our first response should not be a critical remark, but a
supportive one, asking them what they learned from it. Dr.
Loehr, as we saw in Chapter VIII, found that high achieving
athletes accepted their mistakes, made no excuses for them
and learned from them. That's an attitude our kids would do
well to practice.

The "attitude" skills become more significant as the kids
get older in sports. The "mental" game is often what
separates the average athlete from the one who stands out
in any sport. Sometimes, as parents, if our kids want to
continue playing sports beyond the recreational level, it is

helpful to point out the research from Dr. Loehr about the mental approach of top athletes. This is not to pressure our kids to shoot for perfection. It's merely to let them know what it takes, and let them make choices.

Dr. Loehr found 10 major characteristics in the *mental* approach of peak performing athletes:

1. 100% concentration in the moment on what they are doing.

2. A state of total relaxation.

3. A feeling of confidence that they can "do anything".

4. A perception of everything moving in slow motion.

5 A feeling of 100% control and a totally effortless automatic state.

6. During their event, they are void of thoughts of anything other than that which they are doing.

7. They don't bring the mental or emotional experiences of other parts of their lives with them to the event.

8. They don't perform for anyone but themselves: not the crowd, their family or others. They perform for personal enjoyment.

9. They assume full responsibility for their errors. They don't blame equipment, conditions, etc..

10. They describe a routine they follow as a pre-performance behavior pattern. These routines are both external behaviors and internal (thoughts and physiology) behaviors.

A final word about skills: Each youth leaguer should be given the opportunity to become aware of the various skills needed in any given sport. Each youth leaguer should have the opportunity to learn and practice those skills, both physical and mental skills. Obviously, some kids will respond more quickly than others. Some will need more attention than others. If we, as parents, help to teach those skills through positive reinforcement, we can help our kids develop the feeling of control, confidence and self esteem that comes from actually going out and doing something as well as you possibly can.

XIII. Set Reasonable Expectations

Mom: *"Doctor, I think my 11 year old son has the potential to be a professional athlete. What should I do?"*

Doctor: *"Get a second opinion!"*

Unrealistic Parental Expectations

It's amazing to me how, in the early years, kids will go to any extreme to get their parents' approval. There's just something about being able to do something, turn to Mom or Dad, and have them smile, or nod approval, or yell, "Way to go!"

On the other hand I have seen kids in my office who have become depressed, even suicidal, because they just couldn't seem to live up to their parents' *expectations.*

Yet, if there's anything true in youth sports, it is this. Many parents seem to have unrealistic expectations of their kids. Especially in the early years, the kids struggle to meet those expectations, often falling short, and feeling bad. As Dr. Margenau points out, sports should offer parents an opportunity to give unqualified, uncensored, absolute approval to their child just for participating in an activity. He calls it the "apple of my eye" dynamic, whereby the parents communicate that, however the kids perform in an activity, they're great just for participating.

Newspaper articles are filled with "horror stories" of overzealous parents of youth leaguers who seem bent on placing more and more pressure on their kid to perform and excel, only to have the kid eventually quit the sport after "burning out." I recently saw a ten year old boy in my office with his father. Dad was concerned about his son's lack of "desire" in baseball. After dad left the room, the boy, in tears, related how he used to love baseball, but had grown sick of it because his dad, over the past year, had made him take 200 swings a day off the batting tee in his back yard, seven days a week. He said he wanted to spend time with his buddies, but his dad had told him that this was the only way to get to the big leagues! The boy eventually quit baseball, feeling that he had failed his dad.

That's not to say that parents should avoid involvement and encouragement in helping their kids develop skills. This whole book has been advocating parental involvement in youth sports. However, as parents, we need to take stock of what we're expecting.

In my opinion, the unrealistic expectations which we, as parents, may have concerning our kids in youth sports, lie in two areas:

1. Not understanding our kids' physical and emotional capabilities at any given age.

2. Becoming caught up in the fantasy of "fame and fortune" through professional sports or college scholarships.

Physical and Emotional Capabilities of Kids

To keep our expectations reasonable when we think of the physical and emotional abilities of our kids in sports, I think we need to be aware of four areas:

1. **Physical coordination**
2. **Attention span**
3. **Motivation**
4. **Dedication**

Physical Coordination

Dr. Margenau notes that physical coordination develops at highly variable rates, particularly in the earlier years. It may also fluctuate in youngsters from day to day. That's why, in those earlier ages, it is inadvisable to set up a strong regimen of "skills practice" in beginner youth sports. The initial attraction to play sports is "fun" and "action." In T-Ball, it's making contact with the ball off the tee, and running around the bases, or running in the outfield. In soccer, it's kicking the ball and running around the field with all the other kids, following the ball, or following a butterfly! However, I've heard parents complaining about "bee hive" soccer at the beginning level, trying to instruct their kids to "stay in their position on the field," telling them not to run around like a "swarm of bees," following the ball all over the field. The way I see it, six or seven year old soccer players have lots of energy, and they love to run. Asking them to "stand still" on the field while all the action is at the other end, is cruel and inhuman punishment!

In the earlier years, as the kids are beginning to develop coordination, the hope is that they will start to develop skills, but the emphasis has to be on fun while practicing skills. It bears repeating that if there's an emphasis on doing it the "right way," the youngster who may or may not have the physical coordination or emotional control to do things the "right way," may give up, become bored, or feel bad for not being able to do it. Also, as we mentioned in the last chapter, there are moms and dads who spend hours with a six year old trying to get him or her to "swing through the ball" or "follow the soccer ball after kicking it," only to become frustrated and impatient. As parents, we can save a lot of wasted energy and frustration if we remember that, at the early ages, the goal is to make sure the kids have fun in athletic activities, and not to worry about coordination skill levels.

As coordination develops and the kids start moving up in levels, skills will become more of an emphasis. However, we still have to be aware that skills can develop in *spurts*. In fact, some kids who develop skills quickly can reach a plateau in the immediate preteen years, and the other kids may catch up with them. Dr. Margenau reminds us not to become preoccupied with continually pressuring our kids to perfect their skills during those years from ages seven to eleven, because, due to growth spurts and coordination problems, the skills may be put on "hold." I have heard disgruntled parents who have spent a lot of money on sports camps for their eight, nine, and ten year old kids. I have heard them complain that they saw minimal improvement in their kids' skills, and I have heard them take it out on their kids, complaining about all the "wasted money."

Dr. Margenau suggests that parents put off all serious coaching and skills training until their kid is eleven or twelve. Coincidentally, this is the age bracket for the kids in the Little League World Series in Williamsport, Pennsylvania.

A final note about skills and coordination. Many young baseball pitchers' arms have been ruined by throwing curveballs before the arm is "ready." Most coaches feel that a kid can be competitive at this age with a fastball and changeup. While it might be exciting for the kids to be able to "break one off" at the plate, they be sacrificing their high school or college career as a pitcher. It's certainly worth thinking about.

Attention Span

Besides being aware of what we can realistically expect from our kids in terms of the development of physical coordination, we also need to remember their developmental level when it comes to attention span. This is a little more difficult for us to keep in mind, because it's not something we can see. It's obvious to us, as parents, that if a kid does not have the physical coordination to kick a soccer ball consistently, we're not going to practice dribbling! Despite the fact that six and seven year olds' attention spans can be measured in terms of *seconds*, many times we find ourselves lecturing our kids about a specific skill, or the value of practice. There is a TV commercial that really brings this out. It shows a coach with some six or seven year old players. They're all sitting on the bench before a game. The coach is "lecturing" to them about "winning" and sports. As he goes on with his speech, one of the kids points to the ground and says, "Hey! There's a grasshopper!" and the whole team jumps off the bench and swarms around to take a look. The coach throws up his hands, shrugs his shoulders, and walks off. The point for us to remember is that kids at this age are very impulsive, very immediate, and very easily distracted. If we expect anything more, we'll be frustrated and disappointed. Practice with these kids needs to be hands-on, short, full of action, and full of success. And, progress in lengthening the attention span needs to be measured in *very small steps*. A six or seven year old youth leaguer who pays attention to the game for five minutes in a row without chasing a butterfly, waving to friends, or asking for snacks, is showing progress!

In connection with the attention span issue, we also have to be realistic in what we expect young kids (six to seven) to *understand* when we talk to them. In those earlier years, kids are very concrete, and they take things literally. Don't expect them to understand sports jargon. I heard a parent talking about her son's first practice in T-ball baseball. The coach told him to "cover second base." So, he went over to second base and threw his body over the bag, "covering" it! I saw a coach tell one of his seven year olds to "hit the cutoff man." The kid went over and punched the other kid! Before a soccer game, a dad took his seven year old son aside, and told him to remember to "mark a man" during the game. As the game started, the boy picked up some dirt and rubbed it on the shoulder of an opponent, "marking" his man!

The eight, nine, and ten year olds will begin to show more concentration and an increased attention span, but not much more. Also keep in mind that some eight year olds have the attention span of six year olds. It's hard to tell by looking at them. Regardless, practice with these kids once again needs to be fast moving, involving as many senses as possible (visual, sound, touch). Moreover, as soon as the kids in this age bracket get distracted, it's tough to bring them back on track. It takes a lot of effort, and lots of creativity. Once again, coaching and practicing videos can be helpful, but as parents, we have to be very careful lest we overestimate our kids' ability to concentrate on any one skill too long. The ten year old boy mentioned at the beginning of the chapter, whose father made him take 200 swings a day, was being asked to do something well beyond his age in terms of concentration and the ability to handle boredom. The general consensus is that the 11 and 12 year olds have the attention span abilities to stay on task and concentrate on learning their skills.

Motivation

However, there is a world of difference between having the attention span skills to concentrate on a sport, and the motivation to do so! This brings us to the third area of unrealistic expectations: motivation.

I was at a Pop Warner football game of eight year olds. As the second half was starting, the score was 14-0. One of the dads on the losing team yelled out, "Come on you guys! Dig in! You've gotta want it!" I thought to myself, "Want what? What is it that they've 'gotta want'?" Why does an eight year old want to play youth sports? Research shows that, in the early years, kids play organized sports because their parents sign them up to play. There's no inherent love of competition or thrill of winning in the early years. And yet, this dad was expecting these little guys to be motivated to get out there and "give it their all." As was noted in earlier chapters, Dr. Tom Tutko, sports psychologist, talks about *peer involvement* as the main motivation for the kids at ages nine, ten, eleven, twelve in youth sports. The thing that keeps them going in any given sport is their buddies, and team identity. I mentioned in an earlier chapter that my son chose to play soccer rather than baseball one year because his buddies were all playing soccer. As parents, we have to remember the strength of peer pressure in this age group. Dr. Tutko points to the later years, 13 and up, as the age at which kids develop a desire to play *sports for sports sake.*

There are, of course, exceptions to every rule. We've all seen the kid with a burning desire and a total consumption for a given sport, who thrives on practice, competition, or pressure. But these are the exception, and parents need to be aware of the futility of trying to "push" or expect a kid to be totally and absolutely motivated to participate in any given sport.

Dedication

Finally, there's the matter of dedication. How much can we, as parents, expect our kids to be dedicated to reach a specific goal in youth sports? Obviously, in the earlier years this doesn't even come into play. What about those middle or later years? What about the parents who are told that their kid has all-star potential? Is it unrealistic to expect a kid to work hard, in dedicated practice, to hone that special skill? Once again, we have to remember the age. As we have mentioned Dr. Tutko's point repeatedly throughout this book, nine to twelve year olds are more into process than end product. Recalling that ten year old boy noted in the beginning of the chapter, the dad was more interested in the end product of a perfect swing and a high batting average. The boy, if he was going to be interested at all, would have to be interested in the process of swinging the bat. If the daily "200-swings-a-day" practice had been made into some kind of game, with fun, and somehow involving his buddies, he might have responded.

Even at the Olympics level, organizations are rethinking their expectations of the amount of dedication to be expected of pre-teens. Noted sportswriter Frank Carroll points out that the United States Swimming Organization has changed expectations with regard to the amount of dedication expected from eleven year old swimmers. They used to expect 35 hours a week in the pool from potential Olympic hopefuls. However, they realized that, at that age, the kids wanted to play other sports as well, and wanted a social life. They noted that Mike Schmidt (former professional baseball star) and Kiki Vandeweghe (basketball pro) both became burned out swimmers at an early age. The United States Swimming Organization has decided to lessen their expectations of swimmers at age 11, allowing them to play other sports until they reach the age at which dedication sets in.

What about when the age of dedication does set in? Is it realistic for us, as parents, to push for excellence in our kid in a given sport? Dr. Margenau discusses this topic at length, noting that it takes a special kind of *psychological toughness* to dedicate the time necessary to become a top athlete. He warns us to be on the lookout for signs (repeated complaints of stomachaches, headaches, sleep problems, or appetite problems) that our kid, although having the physical skills, may lack the emotional strength to handle the pressure to perform, with excellence, on command.

Keeping our expectations realistic when it comes to our kids' physical and emotional abilities is a real challenge for parents. We've got to check ourselves periodically to make sure that we're aware of our kids' level of coordination, attention span, motivation and dedication. If we do this, we've got a good chance of making sure we're not frustrated and of making sure that our kids are not suffering from being unable to live up to our expectations.

Fantasy of "Fame and Fortune"

Yet, even if we are able to keep our expectations in check with regard to our kids' physical and emotional abilities in youth sports, there's still that other area of unrealistic expectations: the hope, the fantasy, that our talented kid may somehow gain "fame and fortune" through becoming a professional athlete, or at least win an athletic scholarship to college.

It's getting to be almost an everyday occurrence. You pick up a newspaper, you watch TV, you listen to the radio, and what's the big news? A few more athletes have just signed million dollar, or multimillion dollar contracts. The athletes are interviewed; they thank their parents for all their encouragement, and they buy them a new home. Is it any wonder that we find parents attempting, from the earliest stages of sports involvement, to get their kid the best training, the best coach, the best equipment, or the best "contacts" in the hopes of pursuing that magic dream of having their kid become a professional athlete? Some parents seem possessed and preoccupied with this unrealistic dream. They insist that their kid be allowed to play a certain position on a team because it's the position most likely to get their kid noticed. They move to a specific area because it has the best "sports" environment. The entire family centers around preparing for the "dream," and often, as the quote at the beginning of the chapter notes, parents may be unrealistic in their appraisal of their kid's skill.

Even if the kid is talented, the *odds* of becoming a professional athlete are astronomical. In baseball, for example, it has been pointed out that there are literally millions of youngsters playing in thousands of leagues around the country. Many of these kids are good, some are great, and some are truly exceptional. Only the truly exceptional get a shot. As Dr. Margenau points out, there are only 650 positions available in major league baseball (50 more with the two expansion teams in 1993) , and of those only about 10% open up each year. Injuries end careers abruptly, and many players linger in the minor leagues without ever getting to the "bigs."

Most parents would probably agree that a professional athletic career is just a "pipe dream," and once it's pointed out to them they come back to earth rather quickly. However, in these tough economic times, it is understandable that parents may be hoping for some kind of financial aid through an *athletic scholarship*. It's understandable to want to get as much exposure for your kid as possible. It's also understandable to encourage your kid to take up a sport in which colleges are offering increased scholarships.

The issue here is not that we're supposed to abandon all dreams of success for our kids in sports. Dreams and goals are what motivate people. Kids are forever dreaming of being a star, a hero, a winner, a famous athlete. The issue is that as parents, while we're talking of dreams and wishes for our kids in sports, we have to be careful of the *pressure* we may put on the kid to reach the "pot of gold." We have to guard against pressuring our kids into thinking they will be failures if they don't help us fulfill our dreams for them. It's not just pressure on the kid, it's pressure on the whole *family*. It's very important to be aware of the social price we may have to pay if we launch a "promotional campaign" with our kid in sports. I have seen many families in my office which have been torn apart, with strained family relations among family members. I have seen severe cases of sibling rivalry because everything centers around the "athletic" child, to the exclusion of the "less athletic" brothers and sisters. I have seen parents of kids on a team stop socializing with other parents because of an "our kid is much more athletically gifted than your kid" attitude. I've even seen marriages falter because of a relentless, unrealistic "sports career" preoccupation on the part of one spouse which is not shared by the other spouse. I mention all this so that we, as parents, can ask ourselves, as we find ourselves becoming wrapped up the fantasy of "fame and fortune," whether it's all worth it.

Expectations: Don't Overestimate or Underestimate

When we enroll our kids in youth sports, we're hoping that they'll have fun, feel good about themselves, and learn skills to the best of their ability. And that's what our expectations should be based on, a knowledge and awareness of our kids' coordination, attention span, motivation, and dedication, based upon their age and their level of development. If we keep this in mind we will avoid the two extremes:

1. *Underestimating* our kids' abilities: giving them no goals, no challenges, making them feel worthless because we see them as incompetent.

2. *Overestimating* our kids' abilities: giving them goals and challenges beyond their reach, and dooming them to feelings of failure.

Finding that middle ground is an ongoing task for us throughout the youth sports experience. Along the way, we have to remember the important role which our expectations play in developing the self esteem of our youth leaguers.

Epilogue

Volumes have been written about how to enhance a kid's self concept. As a psychologist, father of three, and a youth league coach, I think that youth sports, besides being one of the treasured experiences in life, is a wonderful way to build self confidence in a child. Along the way, it offers the bonus of building positive memories and an opportunity to spend time together as a family unit.

My hope is that this book can offer all parents an opportunity to check on how well they're doing with helping their youth leaguers develop their self esteem through youth sports.

The **Parent Checklist** in the Appendix is not a pass-fail test. It is simply an opportunity for parents to note how well they're using youth sports to promote self esteem in their kids. There will be areas in which a parent is right on track, there may be some areas where they may need an occasional reminder now and then. It never hurts to get out the list at the beginning of each season and to check yourself occasionally during the season.

In closing, I would like to quote Dr. Margenau:

In athletics, there is nothing the child can possibly do that a parent can't convert into a positive event. The idea is to reinforce participation and not to demean the child's efforts for any reason. Athletics provides even the most inept and uncoordinated child with the opportunity to receive parental approval... So, if you can give your child one special feeling, make it the feeling of thinking that he is the best thing that has ever happened to this planet. If you do nothing else as a parent, you will have given a tremendous gift.

Appendix:

Skills & Positive Behavior Checklists

Baseball/Softball Skills Checklist

Hitting

___ 1. Steps into ball.

___ 2. Keeps foot planted.

___ 3. Keeps shoulders level (no upper cut).

___ 4. Grips bat properly.

___ 5. Extends arm completely.

___ 6. Keeps head in "V" position and eyes on the ball.

___ 7. Swings through the ball (follows through).

___ 8. Good, aggressive swing.

Pitching and Throwing

___ 1. Steps in direction of throw.

___ 2. Reaches back far enough to throw.

___ 3. Throws "over the top" (elbow higher than shoulder).

___ 4. Good, accurate throws (good control).

Fielding

___ 1. Bends knees on grounders (stays low).

___ 2. Moves forward on ball (doesn't wait).

___ 3. Fields ball in middle of body.

___ 4. Spreads feet at least shoulder width apart.

___ 5. Gets rid of ball quickly to throw.

___ 6. Uses two hands consistently.

___ 7. Hands "give" with ball (no flipping at it).

Baseball/Softball Positive Behavior
Checklist

__ 1. Hustles out to the field and back to the dugout.
__ 2. Tags up on a fly ball.
__ 3. Throws the ball to the correct base.
__ 4. Throws to the cut-off person.
__ 5. Gets under the ball to catch a fly ball.
__ 6. Gets the ball from outfield to infield quickly.
__ 7. Backs up a throw.
__ 8. Cheers for teammates while on the bench.
__ 9. Keeps up "chatter" on the field.
__ 10. Hustles while running on the bases.
__ 11. Watches the coach for signs.
__ 12. Slides into base on close plays.
__ 13. Encourages teammates ("nice try!").
__ 14. Runs out every hit (grounder, fly ball, or pop up).
__ 15. Keeps track of personal equipment (glove, bat, hat, and ball).
__ 16. Respects team equipment (bats, helmets, and balls).
__ 17. Pays attention to the game (score, outs, and inning).
__ 18. Shows good sportsmanship before, during, and after game.
__ 19. Helps pick up team equipment after practice and game.
__ 20. Comes on time for practice and game.

Basketball Skills Checklist

Shooting

___ 1. Lays ball up softly and jumps off correct foot (layup).

___ 2. Squares shoulders to basket and bends knee slightly.

___ 3. Moves elbow upward and forearm toward basket.

___ 4. Arches ball. Wrist follows through to basket.

Passing

___ 1. Thrusts arms forward and snaps wrists.

___ 2. Uses fingers, not palms.

___ 3. Passes accurately (chest and bounce pass).

___ 4. Doesn't "telegraph" pass (uses fakes).

Dribbling

___ 1. Doesn't look at ball while dribbling.

___ 2. Uses either hand.

___ 3. Pushes (doesn't slap) ball to floor with fingers.

Rebounding

___ 1. "Blocks out" on defense.

___ 2. Passes to "outlet" player after defensive rebound.

___ 3. Moves to get "position" for offensive rebound.

Pivoting

___ 1. Keeps rear foot in contact with floor.

Defense

___ 1. Keeps head up, looking at opponent's midrift.

___ 2. Bends knee slightly.

___ 3. Remains between opponent and basket.

___ 4. Keeps hands moving (both up, or one up/one down).

Basketball Positive Behavior
Checklist

___ 1. Hustles after the loose ball.

___ 2. Goes to the basket for rebounds.

___ 3. Lets hands "give" when receiving the ball (soft hands).

___ 4. Exhales deep breath before shooting foul shot.

___ 5. Passes to receiver on side away from defensive player.

___ 6. Moves around the court without the ball on offense.

___ 7. Makes accurate chest pass (above waist, below head).

___ 8. Gets down court quickly on offense and defense.

___ 9. Passes to "open" player.

___ 10. Stays in assigned position on offense and defense.

___ 11. Listens to coach (during game and time-outs).

___ 12. Controls temper.

___ 13. Cheers for team while on bench.

___ 14. Encourages teammates ("nice try!").

___ 15. Keeps track of personal equipment (uniform, ball, and shoes).

___ 16. Respects team equipment (balls, towels, and scorebook).

___ 17. Pays attention to game (score, quarter, and time left).

___ 18. Shows good sportsmanship before, during, and after game.

___ 19. Helps pick up team equipment after practice and game.

___ 20. Comes on time for practice.

Football Skills Checklist

Blocking

___ 1. Aligns body with opponent.
___ 2. Looks straight ahead when in stance.
___ 3. Contacts with shoulders and upper arms.
___ 4. Drives legs with short choppy steps.

Tackling

___ 1. Keeps head up and eyes on runner's midsection.
___ 2. Drives shoulder into runner with head to the outside.
___ 3. Locks hands and wrists around runner's legs.
___ 4. Follows through, driving with legs.

Running

___ 1. Looks stright ahead when in stance.
___ 2. Tucks ball in and carries it on correct side of body.
___ 3. Keeps legs moving, with high knee kicks.

Passing

___ 1. Throws with overhead motion.
___ 2. Points front foot toward target.
___ 3. Shifts weight to front at time of release.
___ 4. Follows through.

Receiving

___ 1. Keeps eye on ball at time of reception.
___ 2. Catches with hands, not body.
___ 3. Hands "give" when receiving the ball.

Football Positive Behavior
Checklist

__ 1. Hustles on field and off.

__ 2. Blocks the assigned opponent.

__ 3. Runs a "clean" pass pattern.

__ 4. Gives a "second effort" on a block or tackle.

__ 5. Hustles until whistle blows on each play.

__ 6. Covers assigned opponent or zone on defense.

__ 7. Hustles to recover a fumble.

__ 8. Hustles back to huddle.

__ 9. Listens to cadence of signals on offense or defense.

__ 10. Listens in the huddle.

__ 11. Keeps up "chatter" on the field.

__ 12. Cheers from the sidelines.

__ 13. Listens to the coach.

__ 14. Keeps eyes straight ahead when lining up on offense.

__ 15. Keeps track of personal equipment (mouthpiece, and helmet).

__ 16. Respects team equipment (balls, tees, and uniform).

__ 17. Pays attention to game (score, quarter, downs, and time left).

__ 18. Shows good sportsmanship before, during, and after game.

__ 19. Helps pick up team equipment after practice and game.

__ 20. Comes on time for practice and game.

Soccer Skills Checklist

Kicking

___ 1. Looks at target while approaching ball.
___ 2. Keeps eye on ball at time of kick.
___ 3. Kicks with full contact on inside of foot.
___ 4. Follows through in intended direction.

Passing

___ 1. Accuracy: reaches target.
___ 2. Power: maintains appropriate speed of ball.
___ 3. Timing: releases when player is "open".
___ 4. Disguise: uses body and head fakes.

Dribbling

___ 1. Keeps ball close to feet.
___ 2. Controls and varies ball speed.
___ 3. Controls without always looking at ball.

Throw-ins

___ 1. Keeps both hands on ball.
___ 2. Releases from over the head.
___ 3. Keeps both feet on the ground.

Heading

___ 1. Uses forehead.
___ 2. Keeps eye on ball at time of contact.
___ 3. Coordinates feet, legs, trunk, and neck.

Trapping

___ 1. Keeps eye on approaching ball.
___ 2. Relaxes and pulls back trapping body part on contact.

Soccer Positive Behavior
Checklist

__ 1. Hustles on the field and off.

__ 2. Goes to the ball.

__ 3. Throws in rapidly to open player.

__ 4. Avoids "offside" penalties.

__ 5. On defense, stays between attacking player and goal.

__ 6. Follows up on kicks.

__ 7. Moves without the ball to get open.

__ 8. Calls out player/ball location to teammates ("man on!").

__ 9. Kicks with either foot.

__ 10. Cheers for teammates while on sidelines.

__ 11. Encourages teammates ("nice try!").

__ 12. Pays attention to game (score, quarter, and time).

__ 13. Hustles after loose ball.

__ 14. Stays in position.

__ 15. Pays attention to coach during practice and game.

__ 16. Shows good sportsmanship before, during, and after game.

__ 17. Keeps track of personal equipment (ball, and shoes).

__ 18. Respects team equipment after practice and game.

__ 19. Helps pick up team equipment after practice and game.

__ 20. Comes on time for practice and game.

86 Ways to Say "Very Good"

1. Good for you!
2. Superb.
3. You did that very well.
4. You've got it made.
5. Terrific!
6. That's not bad!
7. Couldn't have done it better myself.
8. Marvelous!
9. You're doing fine.
10. You're really improving.
11. You're on the right track now!
12. Now you've figured it out.
13. Outstanding!
14. That's coming along nicely.
15. I knew you could do it.
16. Good work
17. You figured that out fast.
18. I think you've got it now.
19. I'm proud of the way you worked today.
20. Tremendous!
21. You certainly did well today.
22. Perfect!
23. Nice going.
24. You've got your brain in gear today.
25. Now you've got the hang of it.
26. WOW!
27. Wonderful!
28. You're getting better every day.
29. You're learning fast.
30. You make it look easy.
31. That's a good boy/girl.
32. That's very much better.
33. Super!
34. You did a lot of work today!
35. Keep it up!
36. You've got that down pat.
37. Congratulations.
38. Exactly right!
39. Nice going.
40. Excellent!
41. Sensational!
42. You're doing beautifully.
43. You've just about mastered that!
44. That's really nice.
45. That's the best ever.
46. That's great.

47. Way to go!
48. That's the way to do it!
49. That's quite an improvement.
50. Good thinking.
51. You're really going to town.
52. Keep up the good work.
53. That's it!
54. That's better.
55. You haven't missed a thing.
56. Fantastic!
57. You outdid yourself today!
58. You're doing a good job.
59. That's the right way to do it.
60. That's better.
61. Right on!
62. Well, look at you go!
63. That's the best you've ever done.
64. That's RIGHT!
65. You must have been practicing!
66. Great!
67. Keep working on it; you're getting better.
68. You remembered!
69. That kind of work makes me very happy.
70. You're really working hard today.
71. That's what I call a fine job!
72. I knew you could do it!
73. I'm very proud of you.
74. One more time and you'll have it.
75. Fine!
76. That's good.
77. Good job.
78. You really make this fun.
79. Good remembering.
80. Nothing can stop you now.
81. You are doing much better today.
82. Keep on trying.
83. You are really learning a lot.
84. You've just about got it.
85. I've never seen anyone do it better.
86. You are very good at that.

(Reprinted with special permission from Growing Parent. *January, 1985. Vol. 13, #1)*

Kids, Sports, and Self Esteem:
Parent Checklist

Grade yourself on each of the following 20 items.
(0 = Never   1 = Sometimes   2 =Always)

___   1. I praise my kids just for participating in sports, regardless of their athletic skills.

___   2. I try to make sure my kids feel that they belong in our family, regardless of their athletic skills.

___   3. I remind my kids that they are worthwhile as persons, regardless of athletic skills.

___   4. I treat my kids with respect, avoiding put-downs, sarcasm, or ridicule, on the field or off.

___   5. I help my kids develop a feeling of being in control in sports, helping them develop skills through practice.

___   6. I remember to look for, and make a "big deal" out of positives with my kids, on and off the field.

___   7. I help my kids recognize even their smallest progress in Youth Sports activities.

___   8. I praise my kids for specific behaviors, keeping a four to one ratio of positives to negatives, on the field and off.

___   9. I remain calm when my kids make a mistake, on the field or off, helping them learn from their mistakes.

___ 10. I remind my kids not to get down on themselves when things aren't going well in Youth Sports.

__ 11. I remember not to take myself too seriously when it comes to my involvement in youth sports.

__ 12. I remind myself to laugh and keep a sense of humor, on the field and off.

__ 13. I remind my kids to laugh and keep a sense of humor, on the field and off.

__ 14. I emphasize teamwork and a team identity in team youth sports.

__ 15. I help my kids think "we" instead of "me".

__ 16. I try to "get into my kids' shoes," and see youth sports through the eyes of my youth leaguers.

__ 17. I get involved and show an interest in my kids' sports activities.

__ 18. I keep my expectations reasonable when it comes to my kids, on the field and off.

__ 19. I show my kids a good example of sportsmanship and self esteem.

__ 20. I maintain a "Fun is Number One" attitude in youth sports.

References

Branden, Nathaniel. (1992). *The Power of Self Esteem*. Deerfield Beach, FL: Health Communications, Inc.

Burnett, Darrell. (1991). *The Art of Being a Successful Youth League Manager-Coach (Baseball/Softball)*. Laguna Niguel, CA: Funagain Press. P.O. Box 7223. Laguna Niguel, CA. 92607-7223.

Burnett, Darrell. (1991). *The Art of Being a Successful Youth League Manager-Coach (Basketball)*. Laguna Niguel, CA: Funagain Press. P.O. Box 7223. Laguna Niguel, CA. 92607-7223.

Burnett, Darrell. (1991). *The Art of Being a Successful Youth League Manager-Coach (Football)*. Laguna Niguel, CA: Funagain Press. P.O. Box 7223. Laguna Niguel, CA. 92607-7223.

Burnett, Darrell. (1991). *The Art of Being a Successful Youth League Manager-Coach (Soccer)*. Laguna Niguel, CA: Funagain Press. P.O. Box 7223. Laguna Niguel, CA. 92607-7223.

Burnett, Darrell. (1991) *The Art of Being a Successful Youth League Manger-Coach: 14 Steps*. Audiotape. Laguna Niguel, CA: Funagain Press. P.O. Box 7223, Laguna Niguel, CA. 92607-7223.

Burnett, Darrell. (1991). *Parents, Kids, and Self Esteem: 15 Ways to Help Kids Like Themselves.* Audiotape. Laguna Niguel, CA: Funagain Press. P.O. Box 7223. Laguna Niguel, CA 92607-7223.

Burnett, Darrell. (1991).*Raising Responsible Kids: 5 Steps for Parents.* Audiotape. Laguna Niguel, CA: Funagain Press. P.O. Box 7223. Laguna Niguel, CA 92607-7223.

Burnett, Darrell. (1992). *Improving Parent-Adolescent Relationships: Learning Activities for Parents and Adolescents.* Leader Manual and Participant Workbook. Muncie, IN: Accelerated Development, Inc., Publishers.

California Task Force to Promote Self Esteem and Personal and Social Responsiblity. (1990). *Toward a State of Esteem: The Final Report of the California Task Force to Promote Self Esteem and Personal and Social Responsibility.* (1990). Sacramento, CA: Bureau of Publications, California State Department of Education.

Canfield, Jack, and Wells, Harold. (1976). *100 Ways to Enhance Self Concept in the Classroom: A Handbook for Teachers and Parents.* Englewood Cliffs, New Jersey: Prentice-Hall, Inc.

Carroll, Frank. (June 25, 1991). "Pressure Parents Exert Can Negate Value of Youth Leagues." *Orlando Sentinel,* printed in the *San Diego Union.* P.O. Box 191. San Diego, CA. 92112-4106.

Clemes, Harris & Bean, Reynold. (1990). *How to Raise Children's Self Esteem.* Los Angeles, CA: Price Stern Sloan, Inc.

Coopersmith, Stanley. (1981). *The Antecedents of Self Esteem.* Palo Alto, CA: Consulting Psychologists Press, Inc.

Cousins, Norman . (1980). *Anatomy of an Illness.* Boston: G.K. Hall.

Geist, William. (1992). *Little League Confidential: One Coach's Completely Unauthorized Tale of Survival.* New York: Macmillan.

Gibbons, Amy. (Spring 1992). "Why do Kids Play Sports?"*Sportscene* Vol. 23, No. 2. Newsletter of the Southern California Municipal Athletic Federation. P.O. Box 3605. South El Monte, CA 91733.

Loehr, James. (1982). *Mental Toughness Training for Sports. Achieving Athletic Excellence.* Lexington, MA: Stephen Greene Press.

Margenau, Eric. (1990). *Sports Without Pressure. A Guide for Parents and Coaches of Young Athletes.* New York: Brunner/Mazel, Inc.

Michener, James. (1976). *Sports in America.* New York: Random House.

McInally, Pat. (1988). *Moms & Dads & Kids & Sports* New York: Charles Scribner's Sons.

McIntosh, Ned. (1985). *Managing Little League Baseball.* Chicago, IL: Contemporary Books, Inc.

Sewell, Dan. (Fall, 1992). "Are Parents Ruining the Games?" *Youth Sports Coach.* Newsletter published by the National Youth Sports Coaches Association. 261 Old Okeechobee Rd. West Palm Beach, FL 33409.

Tutko, Thomas and Bruns, William. (1976). *Winning is Everything and Other American Myths.* New York: Macmillan.

Tutko, Thomas, Ph.D. (Summer 1989) "Sports Psychology: The Newsletter for Concerned Coaches, Parents, and Athletes" *Athletic Directory,* 20622 Ottawa Road, Apple Valley, CA 92308.

Waitley, Denis. (1988). *How to Build Your Child's Self Esteem*. Audiotape Seminar. Chicago, IL: Nightingale Conant.

Coaching Aids

The ESPN Youth Coaching Series (Videotapes): *Teaching Kids Basketball with John Wooden, Teaching Kids Football with Bo Schembechler, Teaching Kids Soccer with Bob Gansler*. Maple Plain, MN: Sybervision Systems, Inc. P.O. Box 2276. Maple Plain, MN. 55348. (800) 678-0887.

A Coaching Clinic. (1991). Major League Baseball Home Video. Major League Baseball Properties, Inc. The Phoenix Communications Group, Inc. Distributed by Major League Baseball Productions.

Your Best Shot. Shooting the Basketball for High Percentage. (1987). Videotape. Scholarships Basketball, LTD.

National Youth Sports Organizations:

National Youth Sports Coaches Association
2611 Old Okeechobee Road
West Palm Beach, FL 33409
(407) 684-1141

Baseball
Little League Baseball Incorporated
International Headquarters
P.O. Box 3485
Williamsport, PA 17701
(717) 326-1921

Softball

Bobby Sox Softball
National Headquarters
P.O. Box 5880
Buena Park, CA 90622
(714) 522-1234

Amateur Softball Association of America
Junior Olympics Program
2801 N. E. 50th Street
Oklahoma City, OK 73111
(405) 424-5266

Basketball

National Junior Basketball Association
National Headquarters
1117 W. Orangethorpe
Fullerton, CA 92633

Football

Pop Warner Football
National Headquarters
1315 Walnut St., Suite 1632
Philadelphia, PA 19107
(215) 735-1450

Junior All American Football

811 Handy Street

Orange, CA 92667

(714) 639-4451

Soccer

American Youth Soccer Association

National Headquarters

5403 W. 138th Street

Hawthorne, CA 90250

(800) 872-2976

(213) 643-6455

United States Youth Soccer Association, Inc.

Campbell Business Center

2050 N. Plano Road, Suite 100

Richardson, TX 75082

(800) 4-SOCCER

(214) 235-4499

Soccer Association for Youth

4903 Vine Street

Cincinnati, OH 45217

(513) 242-4263

National Youth Organizations

YMCA of the USA
40 West Long Street
Columbus, OH 43215

Boys and Girls Clubs of America
771 First Avenue
New York, NY 10017

ABOUT THE AUTHOR

Dr. Darrell Burnett is a clinical child psychologist, a youth league coach, a certified sports psychologist specializing in youth sports, and the father of three.

As a clinical psychologist he has been in private practice in southern California (Laguna Niguel) for 20 + years. He has been interested in "positive parenting" issues throughout his professional career. He has worked as a teacher, a program director of adolescent and children psychiatric services, and as a consultant to schools, social service agencies, probation departments, military bases, business corporations, and hospitals. He is the author of a manual and workbook, **Improving Parent-Adolescent Relationships**, and two audiotape seminars with booklets, **Raising Responsible Kids: 5 Steps for Parents**, and **Parents, Kids, & Self-Esteem: 15 Ways to Help Kids Like Themselves**.

As a youth sports psychologist, Dr. Burnett, a member of the National Speakers Association, is active on the lecture circuit. He was the keynote speaker at the Rhode Island Scholar-Athlete Games, sponsored by the Institute for International Sport, at the University of Rhode Island. The Institute elected him as a National Sports Ethics Fellow, recognizing his "consistent interest and effort in promoting the ideals of ethics and fair play in sports and society." *USA Today* published his article on "Parents and Sportsmanship" as part of National Sportsmanship Day. He was the keynote speaker at five sectional conferences for the American Youth Soccer Organization (AYSO). He was the luncheon keynote speaker at the Western Regional Little League Tournament. At a youth sports clinic sponsored by the Los Angeles Kings Hockey, he addressed parents on the topic "The Role of Parents in Their Child's Sports Career". He is a frequent guest speaker at youth sports coaching clinics discussing positive coaching. He continues to present seminars for city, state, and regional conferences of the Parks and Recreation Association.

Dr. Burnett has been quoted as a youth sports expert in several issues of *Sports Illustrated*. He has appeared on numerous local and national radio and TV programs. He has been interviewed on several Internet chat rooms (ESPN.com, USAToday.com, etc.)

Besides writing numerous magazine, newspaper, and Internet articles, Dr. Burnett has several publications in the area of youth sports: *The Art of Being a Successful Youth League Coach*. (A *positive coaching* booklet series with audio tape); "*Hey, Mom & Dad, It's Just a Game!*" (An audiotape guide discussing his Sport Parent Attitude & Behavior Checklist); *Kids & Tee-Ball: What's a Parent to Do?* in *The Official T-Ball USA Family Guide to Tee Ball*; *A Coach with Soul*, in *Chicken Soup for the Soul at Work*; and *Challenger Baseball*, in *Chicken Soup for the Unsinkable Soul*. He was also a primary author in the Gatorade *Playbook for Kids: A Parent's Guide To Help Kids Get the Most Out of Sports.*

Dr. Burnett has also applied the sports analogy to the corporate world in his booklet and audiotape: *The Positive Corporate Manager: Lessons from Coaching Kids* (*How To Build Employee Self-Esteem in the Workplace*). In his corporate workshops, he shows how the manager, as "coach", can build employee self-esteem and productivity in the workplace.

As a youth league coach, Dr. Burnett has coached Little League baseball, AYSO soccer, and National Junior Basketball. Since 1991 he has coached developmentally disabled youngsters, and served as a District Commissioner for the Little League Baseball "Challenger" Program for disabled youngsters. He also coaches developmentally disabled youngsters in soccer ("VIP", AYSO), & basketball ("Hot Hoops", NJB).

Visit Dr. Burnett's website at www.djburnett.com.

AFTERWORD

YOUTH HOCKEY SKILLS CHECKLIST

YOUTH HOCKEY POSITIVE BEHAVIOR CHECKLIST

PLAYER SPORTSMANSHIP CHECKLIST

PARENT SPORTSMANSHIP CHECKLIST

"SIDELINE SUGGESTIONS"

UPDATED REFERENCES

YOUTH HOCKEY SKILLS CHECKLIST

Ready Position
_____1. Knees bent over toes.
_____2. Skates shoulder width apart.
_____3. Back, chest, & head up, looking forward.

Holding the Stick
_____1. V grip with thumb and forefinger.
_____2. Top hand (control) at taped end of stick shaft.
_____3. Bottom hand (power) 8"-14" below top hand.
_____4. Top elbow away from body.

Shooting
_____1. Looks at target.
_____2. Transfers weight from back to front.
_____3. Snaps wrists.
_____4. Follows through, with toe of blade toward target.
_____5. Accuracy: on goal.
_____6. Timing: shoots when an opening is available.

Passing
_____1. Accuracy: passes to teammate's stick; leads teammate.
_____2. Power: maintains appropriate puck speed.
_____3. Timing: releases when player is open.
_____4. Disguise: uses head and body fakes (doesn't telegraph pass).
_____5. Transfers weight from back to front.
_____6. Follows through, with toe of blade toward target.

Stick Handling
_____1. Keeps stick in front of body.
_____2. Uses short, quick strokes.
_____3. Keeps puck in front and within range.
_____4. Rolls wrist toward surface.
_____5. Pushes and pulls (doesn't slap).
_____6. Controls without looking at puck (uses split vision).

YOUTH HOCKEY POSITIVE BEHAVIOR CHECKLIST

_____1. Hustles onto and off the rink.

_____2. Continues to move around the rink without the puck.

_____3. On defense, stays between attacking player and goal.

_____4. Lets stick "give" when receiving the puck.

_____5. Pushes and pulls puck, doesn't slap it.

_____6. Shouts puck/player location to teammates during the game.

_____7. Shows good sportsmanship before, during, and after game.

_____8. Uses body to shield opponent from puck.

_____9. Cheers for teammates while not in game.

_____10. Shoots/passes/stick handles with forehand and backhand.

_____11. Looks for and passes to open teammates.

_____12. Encourages teammates ("Nice try!")

_____13. Maintains game awareness (time, score, etc.)

_____14. Always looks to get open, prepared to receive a pass.

_____15. Pays attention to coach during game and practice.

_____16. Controls temper.

_____17. Keeps track of personal equipment (skates, stick, etc.)

_____18. Respects team equipment.

_____19. Learns from mistakes. Doesn't pout.

_____20. Comes on time for practice and game.

PLAYER SPORTSMANSHIP CHECKLIST
by Darrell J. Burnett, Ph.D.

1.   ___ I abide by the rules of the game.

2.   ___ I try to avoid arguments.

3.   ___ I share in the responsibilities of the team.

4.   ___ I give everyone a chance to play according to the rules.

5.   ___ I always play fair.

6.   ___ I follow the directions of the coach.

7.   ___ I respect the other team's effort.

8.   ___ I offer encouragement to my teammates.

9.   ___ I accept the judgment calls of the game officials.

10.   ___ I end the game smoothly.

Sportsmanship: *The ability 1) to win without gloating, 2) to lose without complaining, and 3) to treat your opponent with respect.*

Sportsmanship Tips
* If you make a mistake, don't pout or make excuses. Learn from your mistakes, and be ready to continue to play.
* If a teammate makes a mistake, offer encouragement, not criticism.
* If you win, don't rub it in.
* If you lose, don't make excuses.

PARENT SPORTSMANSHIP CHECKLIST
by Darrell J. Burnett, Ph.D.

1. __ I maintain a "Fun is Number One" attitude in youth sports.

2. __ I treat officials, coaches, my kids, their teammates, & their opponents with respect, avoiding put-downs, ridicule, or sarcasm, on and off the field.

3. __ I praise my kids, their teammates, and their opponents, just for participating, regardless of their athletic skills.

4. __ I remember to look for, and make a "big deal" out of positives with my kids, their teammates, and their opponents, on and off the field.

5. __ I remain calm when my kids or their teammates make a mistake, on and off the field, helping them learn from their mistakes.

6. __ I remind my kids and their teammates not to get down on themselves when things don't go well in youth sports.

7. __ I try not to take myself too seriously when it comes to my involvement in youth sports.

8. __ I remind myself and my kids to laugh and keep a sense of humor. On and off the field, reminding myself that there is life beyond youth sports.

9. __ I emphasize teamwork in team sports with my kids, teaching them to think "we" instead of "me."

10. __ I teach my kids by giving them an example of good sportsmanship: winning without gloating, losing without complaining, and treating opponents and officials with fairness, generosity, and courtesy.

"SIDELINE SUGGESTIONS"
(10 Things Kids Say They <u>Don't</u> Want From Their Parents)
by Darrell J. Burnett, Ph.D.

1. **Don't yell out instructions.** During the game I'm trying to concentrate on what the coach says, and working on what I've been practicing. It's easier for me to do my best if you save instructions and reminders for practice or just before the game.

2. **Don't put down the officials.** This embarrasses me and I sometimes wonder whether the official is going to be tougher on me because my parents yell.

3. **Don't yell at me in public.** It will just make things worse because I'll be upset, embarrassed, or worried that you're going to yell at me the next time I do something wrong.

4. **Don't yell at the coach.** When you yell about who gets to play what position, it just stirs things up and takes away from the fun.

5. **Don't put down my teammates.** Don't make put-down remarks about my teammates who make mistakes. It takes away from our team spirit.

6. **Don't put down the other team.** When you do this you're not giving us a very good example of sportsmanship so we get mixed messages about being "good sports."

7. **Don't lose your cool.** I love to see you get excited about the game, but there's no reason to get so upset that you lose your temper. It's our game and all the attention is supposed to be on us.

8. **Don't lecture me about mistakes after the game.** Those rides home in the car after the game are not a good time for lectures about how I messed up -- I already feel bad. We can talk later, but please stay calm and don't forget to mention the things I did well during the game!

9. **Don't forget how to laugh and have fun.** Sometimes it's hard for me to relax and have fun during the game when I look over and see you so tense and worried.

10. **Don't forget that it's just a game!** Odds are, I'm not going to make a career out of playing sports. I know I may get upset if we lose, but I also know that I'm usually feeling better after we go get a pizza. I need to be reminded sometimes that it's just a game.

Reprinted with permission from the **Playbook for Kids: A Parent's Guide to Help Kids Get the Most Out of Sports**. (The Gatorade Company)

UPDATED REFERENCES

Clifford, Craig, and Feezell, Randolf (1997). *Coaching for Character*. Champaign, IL: Human Kinetics.

Engh, Fred. (1999). *Why Johnny Hates Sports*. New York, NY: Penguin USA.

Kuchenbecker, Shari. (2000). *Raising Winners: A Parent's Guide to Helping Kids succeed on and off the Playing Field*. New York, NY: Times Books, Random House, Inc.

Murphy, Shane, Ph.D. (1999) *The Cheers and the Tears*. San Francisco, CA: Jossey-Bass Publishers.

Smith, Ronald, and Smoll, Frank. (1996). *Way to Go, Coach!* Portola Valley, CA: Warde Publishers, Inc.

Thompson, James (1995). *Positive Coaching: Building Character and Self-Esteem Through Sports*. Portola Valley, CA: Warde Publishers, Inc.

Wilson, Susan. (2000). *Sports Her Way. Motivating Girls to Start and Stay with Sports*, New York, NY: A Fireside Book, Simon and Schuster, Inc.

Printed in the United States
64449LVS00003B/104